THE AMERICAN NAVIES
of the
REVOLUTIONARY WAR

THE AMERICAN NAVIES

of the

REVOLUTIONARY WAR

Paintings by NOWLAND VAN POWELL

with descriptive notes by the artist

Introduction by Richard B. Morris

G.P. Putnam's Sons New York

Dedicated to
Rear Admiral Ernest McNeill Eller, U.S.N., Ret.
The Director of Naval History when the great
work commenced of compiling and editing the
Naval Documents of the American Revolution

Contents

7

Introduction

Introduction

by Richard B. Morris

Gouverneur Morris Professor Emeritus of History, Columbia University

THE VICTORY of the Thirteen United States in the American Revolution in effect turned the world upside down. It proved not only that a colonial people could rule themselves according to novel republican principles but that they could marshal and somehow keep in being an effective fighting force, and, in a war of endurance and attrition, outlast a great world power. In that epochal struggle fought on sea as well as on land, the ships, their commanders, and their crews played a significant role from almost moments after Lexington and Concord down to the signing of the Preliminary Peace of Paris.

One might, indeed, describe the naval history of the American Revolution as a nautical version of David and Goliath. Except perhaps for that comparatively brief period when the French Navy was effectively committed and boldly directed to advancing the military and amphibious operations of the allied forces in America, the British Navy enjoyed an overwhelming superiority over the tiny Continental fleet, even when Congress' navy was complemented by the naval vessels of individual states and the privateers.

It might be argued that British strategy determined the role to be played by the American Navy in the Revolutionary War. Had the British government taken the advice of its Secretary at War, Viscount Barrington, it would have withdrawn the army of occupation following Lexington and Concord, leaving the rebellious colonies to be dealt with by His Britannic Majesty's navy, redoubtable by tradition if somewhat tarnished and shopworn under the administration of the Earl of Sandwich, the First Lord of the Admiralty. Barrington would have blocked the ports, seized the rebel ships, and interdicted commerce and the fisheries. As late as August 8, 1775, he wrote Lord North, "My own opinion always has been and still is, that the Americans may be reduced by the fleet, but never can be by the army."

The British government's initial reaction to Patriot demonstrators suggested that a naval blockade might be the preferred strategy. In late March of 1774 Parliament had enacted the first of the "Intolerable Acts," this one sealing off the port of Boston and prohibiting trade in and out of the port until the customs had been compensated for the losses incurred in the Boston Tea Party. Just a year later the Restraining Act forbade the New England colonies from trading with any nation but Britain and the British West Indies and barring New Englanders from the North Atlantic fisheries. Two weeks later the provisions of the act were made to apply to most of the other colonies as well.

For these acts to have constituted punishing blows a huge naval force would have had to be dispatched to American waters. However, Sandwich, pursuing the King's own wishes for a land force to subdue rebellion, sent troop transports to North America while husbanding British naval strength in European waters. Contrariwise, Barrington opposed stripping Great Britain of her troops and wanted the major naval forces deployed to lay down a tight naval blockade on the coast.

Had the government heeded Barrington and concentrated on blockade operations, the Patriots would perforce have been compelled to initiate a very different naval strategy from that which they in fact pursued. To develop evasive tactics, a phantom fleet of lightly armed sloops, smacks, shallops, and cutters might have been substituted for larger and more heavily armed vessels, and the problem of procuring desperately needed supplies, either from France directly or by way of the Dutch-held West Indian island of Saint Eustatius might have proved critical. Thus, the insurgent Americans would have been reduced on the seas to a defensive role, and one could speculate that they might have achieved no more success than the Confederate blockade-runners did during the American Civil War. To be sure, a blockade of a sort was sporadically sustained by the British Navy. A naval force blocking the Hudson and astride the Delaware and Chesapeake Bays could, and at times did, interdict North-South communications by the Patriots, transportation as well by water as by land, with the result that some of the Patriot vessels built upriver were never able to get out to open waters and service on the sea.

Instead of instituting a really tight blockade, the British concentrated on an invasion in force of the North American continent at strategic points. The long supply line needed to maintain the Redcoats and Hessians dictated a constant movement of cargo vessels, often in convoys, thereby diverting British fighting ships from other duties and providing the rebel naval forces with a tempting target. Utilizing French ports, American armed vessels made daring forays upon the coasts of the British Isles, bringing terror to the inhabitants of port towns and embarrassment to His Britannic Majesty's home fleet. Nor were the island possessions of the British from Bermuda to the Caribbean immune from attack. Occasionally, too, the Continental and state navies cooperated with Patriot land forces besieging British-held towns along the American coast.

It is the story of these vastly outnumbered Continental and state naval vessels, reinforced by a huge mosquito fleet of privateers, that this collection of Patriot fighting ships brings home so effectively. Nowland Van Powell has shown himself to be an exceptionally talented marine painter, who, in a spirit of romantic realism, nails to the canvas these ships of the days of wood and sail, some of which were fated never to see service at all while others outran and outgunned the enemy.

Mr. Powell brings us to the shipyards where he shows us frigates in the course of construction, ships like the *Congress* and *Montgomery* being built at the sheltered inland shipyard at Poughkeepsie, New York, or the ill-fated *Virginia*, whose keel was laid on the Chesapeake near Baltimore (see facing page 48). We can almost hear the sawing of the timber, its fastener being driven home, the whining of the revolving grindstone, and we can come close to some of the countless complex operations involved in creating from heavy timbers a thing of beauty and an instrument of destruction. The artist captures, too, the drama of ship against wave and re-creates the romantic wildness of sea battles. Minutely researching the birth, career, and final hours of every ship he has chosen to depict, Mr. Powell manages with his paintbrush to discover, as it were, each vessel's distinct personality, her design, rigging, firepower, and even to give us some feeling for her crews in action. He has invested his fighting ships with that spirit of bravado and adventure which animated both ship designers and commanders.

If the Patriot arm emerged in response to British strategy, its program and policy were not conceived at one stroke but developed empirically, and its administration never could be completely centralized. It was to be expected that after Lexington the embattled province of Massachusetts would seize the initiative. Hardly had the Redcoats a chance to evaluate the significance of their inglorious retreat from Concord when the Patriots of Martha's Vineyard recaptured two sloops taken earlier by H.M.S. *Falcon*. When the rebels at Falmouth (now Portland, Maine) were foiled in their efforts to seize at anchor a British vessel, that ship retaliated by burning the greater part of the town. In early August Captain Linzee's sloop of war *Falcon* cannonaded the town of Gloucester.

Off Rhode Island the man-of-war *Rose* leveled her guns in a threatening gesture against rebellious townspeople. To counter the peril that colony commissioned the *Katy* in June, 1775, command of which was given to Captain Abraham Whipple. The Bermuda clipper, so highly prized by John Paul Jones, was to be incorporated into the Continental Navy as the *Providence*, and until it was lost in the ill-planned Penobscot foray it outsailed and outfought the enemy, bringing home a cluster of prizes. Rhode Island, with its greatly exposed seacoast, could hardly be expected to go it alone. On August 26, 1775, that colony's revolutionary legislature called on the Continental Congress to superintend the construction of an "American fleet." Relief did not arrive in time to prevent the *Rose* from subjecting Bristol to an hour and a half's bombardment to back up her commander's demands for some forty head of sheep. Whether the *Rose's* objective was to intimidate the townsfolk or level the town as an example to other noncomplying rebels, her marksmanship, according to a popular contemporary ballad, seemed off target.

> They fired low, they fired high,
> The women scream, the children cry,
> And all their firing and their racket
> Shot off the topmast of a packet!

State navies perforce sprang up to defend territorial waters. Nor were they confined to maritime New England. South Carolina, for example, had fifteen sizable armed ships, some like the notable *Defense* (facing page 34) the equal in size to those of the Continental Navy, and comparable in firepower was the 26-gun frigate *Protector,* launched by Massachusetts in 1779, and victor in a duel with the 32-gun *Admiral Duff* off the coast of Newfoundland (facing page 112).

On occasion the Continental Army was forced to engage in naval operations. The most notable example was the first Continental naval force, which was set up by George Washington. The General, whom Congress had named on June 15, 1775, to command the Continental forces then ringing British-held Boston, could not afford to await a specific directive from Congress before acquiring a small fleet of his own, manned by sea-trained army officers. Acting on the sound advice of that renowned Marblehead seafarer, Colonel John Glover, who was to play so signal a role in transporting Washington's army across inland waters, the General commissioned Captain Nicholas Broughton in September, 1775, to arm and outfit the schooner *Hanna,* the first armed vessel in the service of "the United Colonies of North America" and appropriately the first subject of a painting in Mr. Powell's series (facing page 22). Washington soon augmented his fleet with four new vessels, with Captain John Manly as commodore. Manly and Captain James Mugford, the latter commissioned by General Artemas Ward, quickly distinguished themselves by capturing prizes with substantial cargoes of war matériel. Mugford was killed in May, 1776, in a hand-to-hand encounter with an enemy force which attempted to board the Continental cruiser *Franklin* as she lay aground off Boston, but his crew, outnumbered ten to one, drove off the attackers, who sustained fearful losses. Manly had more than his share of hard luck. He was obliged to strike the frigate *Hancock,* and then lost a privateer, the *Cumberland,* to a British frigate. With other prisoners he escaped from Barbados, seized a sloop, and finally reached Boston in April, 1779.

Benedict Arnold, military hero long before turning traitor, improvised his own little navy on Lake Champlain to hold off a Canadian invasion. The action at Valcour Bay on October 11, 1776 (facing page 40), in which Arnold's fleet was destroyed, had the result of frustrating the enemy's invasion plans, forcing the British to await the end of winter before trying again. When they did try once more in 1777, the Patriot armed forces were ready for Burgoyne, whose capitulation marked a turning point of the war.

Long before its formal Declaration of Independence, but months after setting up a Continental Army, Congress was forced to act by sea as well as by land. Some delegates considered the very notion of pitting an American naval force against the world's greatest navy as purest fantasy. Others estimated the cost as prohibitive, while Congressional delegates from the Middle and Southern colonies were disinclined to outfit armed vessels ostensibly to protect New England's maritime interests. Against these dissenters the eloquence, drive, and technical knowledge of seafaring matters possessed by John Adams prevailed. Shrewd enough to see the necessity of picking a Southerner, Washington, to head a war Down East, Adams persuaded Congress on October 30, 1775, to appoint a seven-man navy committee authorized to acquire armed vessels "for the protection and defence of the United Colonies." During the next month he drafted a set of "Rules for the Regulation of the Navy." He then pushed through Congress the adoption of procedures for judicial trial for cases of prize and capture, allowing for an appeal to the Congress. All in all, Adams plunged into naval affairs with his customary zesty enthusiasm, and retrospectively viewed his service in maritime business as "the pleasantest part" of four years' attendance at Congress.

Henceforward, the navy, like every other branch of the armed services, was to be run by a Congressional committee. This one was known from January, 1776, to December, 1779, as the Marine Committee, assisted by a Navy Board at Boston and another at Philadelphia to handle the business of acquiring and outfitting the Continental fleet. To each state in turn there were assigned one or more Continental agents to deal directly with ships' captains. To relieve some of the administrative pressure from delegates who were constantly being replaced by their respective states, Congress toward the close of 1779 set up a Board of Admiralty, comprising two delegates from Congress and three commissioners from outside that body. Despite charges of inefficiency and at times of mixing public and private interest, this hydraheaded board functioned almost until the conclusion of the fighting.

Finally, in 1781, Congress set up a Department of Marine, but never picked a Secretary, leaving those duties to be exercised by Robert Morris, who, as Superintendent of Finance, carried on far more than the technical duties of that office and, as Agent of Marine, served as executive head of the navy until the end of the war. As if to underscore the lack of one-man responsibility for running the Continental Navy, Congress conferred on their three commissioners in France, Silas Deane, Arthur Lee, and Benjamin Franklin, supervision over naval operations in European waters. When Deane and Lee were recalled and power consolidated in Franklin's hands, that world-renowned statesman-scientist took sole charge of naval operations overseas. He acquired ships, appointed naval agents, issued letters of marque, and served in effect as consul and judge of admiralty. Considering the lengthy communication gap between Philadelphia and Passy, it may be fairly inferred that throughout the war two virtually independent naval operative heads were conducting Continental operations on the seas. In addition, two commercial agents of Congress, William Bingham in Martinique, and Oliver Pollock out of New Orleans, were acquiring, equipping, and refitting American naval vessels, and carrying on limited naval operations on their own, the former in Caribbean waters, the latter, down the Mississippi and in the waters of the Gulf of Mexico.

What would shape the tradition of the American Navy for many years to come was the decision of Congress' Marine Committee on the choice of fighting ships for the Continental Navy. The heavy ships of the line, running to 150 feet in length, and mounting 60 to 120 guns, were equally extravagant in manpower as in cost of construction and maintenance, since their crews numbered from 450 to 1,000 men. "Too costly," was the way in which William Ellery of the Marine Committee characterized such huge ships. For the same number of men, he pointed out, one could man three or four frigates. Since the aim of the Continental naval arm was to destroy the British carrying trade rather than to bring the fight to His Majesty's Navy, the committee chose the vessel of the class next in size and equipment to the ship of the line. The frigate, running roughly 140 feet long (the Continental frigate *Randolph* [facing page 44], exceeded that length by fifteen feet), and carrying 24 to 50 guns on the main deck, with a raised quarterdeck and forecastle. These swift sailing ships could not only outrun the ships of the line, but, drawing less draught than the latter, could sail close to shore with less chance of running aground, with access to harbors interdicted to the larger vessels by sandbars and shallow approaches.

Having decided on the class of fighting ship, Congress resolved in December, 1775, to construct thirteen frigates to be put to sea in slightly more than three months' time. Contracts were accordingly made with shipyards scattered from Portsmouth, New Hampshire, to Baltimore. The target date proved optimistic, for, as Mr. Powell points out, Congress had to outfit, arm, and in fact transform numerous merchantmen which were incorporated into the fleet. British blockade operations, combined with the loss of New York in the summer of '76 and of Philadelphia the following year, kept all but four of the thirteen frigates ordered from rendering active service as late as 1777. The *Hancock* fell to the enemy, and four others had to be destroyed on the stocks to keep them from falling into British hands.

Still, despite these frustrations the Continental Navy was not entirely confined to single-ship actions, colorful and heroic though such exploits were, but on occasion operated as a combat fleet. As early as the spring of 1776 Esek Hopkins of Rhode Island, who, owing more to the good fortune of being the brother of Stephen Hopkins, chairman of Congress' original Naval Committee, than to exceptional qualifications, had been named to command the Continental Navy. With eight ships, Hopkins swooped down on the Bahamas. A marine corps led by Samuel Nicholas, a Philadelphia tavern owner, led the amphibious operation, looting the town of a prized supply of munitions. Mr. Powell has given us (facing page 30) a pictorial view of this first flotilla in action, including the flagships *Alfred*, the *Columbus*, the *Cabot*, the *Andrea Doria*, and the *Providence*, the first frigates commissioned by the Marine Committee, along with the frigate tender *Fly* and 8-gun schooner *Wasp*.

The naval history of the American Revolution is replete with more than enough heroics to inspire any marine artist, and Mr. Powell rises to the challenge. We see the *Raleigh* attacking the *Druid* (facing page 96), the *Saratoga* capturing the *Charming Molly* (facing page 108), the *General*

Pickering in battle with the *Achilles* (facing page 110), the *Protector* engaged with the *Admiral Duff* (facing page 112), that fight to a draw between the *Trumbull* and the *Watt* (facing page 114), and, most celebrated of all the naval engagements in the war, the fierce fight to the death between the *Bon Homme Richard* and the *Serapis* (facing pages 76, 78, 80). In that epochal struggle witnessed by more than 1,500 spectators from Scarborough and Flamborough head, the eccentric French captain Pierre Landais, in command of the Continental frigate *Alliance,* discharged a series of broadsides into the stern of the *Bon Homme Richard,* evidently motivated by jealousy of John Paul Jones and a desire to win the British prize for himself. That victory was not to be his, since Captain Richard Pearson with his own hand struck his colors and surrendered to John Paul Jones.

Most colorful and most celebrated of all the commanders, Jones was passed over time on end for promotion in favor of inferior naval officers who knew how to capitalize on local pressures and inside political connections. Ruthless, flamboyant, but a master of an audacious stategy which proved so effective against Britain's coast and convoys, Jones has won all the laurels from historians and biographers even though he lost most of the promotions. In fact, other naval commanders, whose frigates Mr. Powell depicts in actions with the enemy, deserve a share of the laurels as well. Captains John Barry, Lambert Wickes, and Nicholas Biddle ranged the Atlantic from Newfoundland to the West Indies, taking prizes and striking punishing blows at British ships of war. And a word, too, should be said on behalf of Captain Gustavus Conyngham, who, though an officer in the Continental Navy, sailed in privateers fitted out in France. Conyngham's seizure of British ships caused an outcry on both sides of the Channel. The French, still technically neutral, jailed him and confiscated his lugger. Another vessel, the *Revenge,* was bought and armed for him. After taking several prizes, he actually refitted his ship in an English port. Again an outcry. This time the French dispatched Conyngham's backer, a Philadelphia merchant named William Hodge, for a short stay in the Bastille. But Conyngham continued uninhibited, his *Revenge* taking some sixty prizes in eighteen months. Captured at last and confined to Plymouth's notorious Mill Prison, he managed to dig his way out, got to France, joined John Paul Jones on the *Alliance,* was later recaptured, and then exchanged, a further career in privateering only frustrated by the ending of the war.

Conyngham's heroics dramatized the role of that important third naval arm, the privateer, which supplemented the battered Continental and state navies. Thousands of New England fishermen, unemployed when the Grand Banks were forbidden waters to them, preferred shipping out on an armed ship which had obtained letters of marque from the Congress or a state to enlisting in the Continental or state navies. The entire profits of privateering were divided among the owners and crews, while Continental officers and crews shared a third of the prize if merchantmen, a half if enemy warships. In fact, to compete with privateers Congress had to upgrade the prize money. Congress commissioned some 1,700 privateers; the states perhaps a greater number. Ranging from 100 to 150 tons, some with as many as twenty guns (of which the 18-gun brig privateer *Montgomery* seen here in action with the *Millern* [facing page 54] is a fine example), and with an average crew of a hundred men, the privateers carried a far more meaningful threat to British commerce than did the few Continental frigates with their occasional forays. It has been estimated that they took some $18 million in prizes as compared with a third of that amount credited to the Continental Navy, and as the latter dwindled toward the last years of the war, privateering burgeoned in scope, volume, and significance.

A word, too, about the crews manning the Continental frigates. They were a motley lot. Jones recalled that the crew on the *Bon Homme Richard* numbered eleven different nationalities. They could be insubordinate and at times even mutinous. A sizable percentage were underage, mere boys. But the hated tradition of impressment associated with the Royal Navy had instilled a fierce patriotism in the bosoms of many of them. Incarcerated in England's Mill Prison, they invariably preferred staying in prison to serving on British men-of-war, and one group of imprisoned seamen drafted a constitution to govern their behavior in prison.

As the curtain is rung down on the War of the American Revolution, the navy expires just as independence is achieved. Out of some fifty to sixty vessels converted or built by Congress, only the frigates *Deane* and *Alliance* had survived as fighting ships by early 1782. Appropriately both are the subjects of the final paintings in Mr. Powell's series. Originally acquired by Silas Deane in France, the *Deane* was named in his honor. An undersized but power-packed frigate commanded by the able Captain Samuel Nicholson for most of her service, the ship suffered a change in name just as her sponsor suffered a fall from grace. When word came that Silas Deane had openly disavowed the Revolutionary cause, Congress renamed his ship the *Hague,* in tribute to valued Dutch support, but before the war's end she was sold out of service.

That left only the 36-gun *Alliance,* a ship which boasted a distinction unique in the annals of the United States Navy. Her crew rose up and relieved her erratic and incompetent commander, Pierre Landais. In effect, Congress ratified the mutiny by supplanting Landais with Captain Barry. The *Alliance*'s running battle with the *Sybil* in March of 1783 was the last recorded naval engagement of a Continental vessel in the war. A preliminary peace with Great Britain had been signed on November 30 of the previous year. In August, 1785, the *Alliance* was sold, a transaction which in fact liquidated the first American Navy, now too weak even to take reprisals against the Barbary corsairs. Playing an intrepid role against overwhelming odds for the eight long years of the American Revolution, that first navy richly merits the tribute which this handsome book conveys.

THE AMERICAN NAVIES
of the
REVOLUTIONARY WAR

The first United States war vessel, the *Hanna*

As Commander in Chief of the American Army, George Washington at the siege of Boston had all points covered except the water side of the city. Here, British ships could come and go at will; often a single ship, unguarded, would enter the harbor. Therefore, he determined to attempt to intercept this supply line with a view to distressing the enemy, and at the same time provide his own forces with munitions from captured British ships.

Accordingly, he proposed a plan to the Provincial Congress of Massachusetts, but when there were no immediate results, he acted on his own, as he had authority from the Continental Congress to do.

In his army the troops from Marblehead were all seafaring men led by Colonel John Glover, afterward to become noted for ferrying the Continental Army across the East River after the Battle of Long Island, and across the Delaware at the Battle of Trenton. The plan was placed before Glover, and acting on his recommendations, General Washington commissioned Nicholas Broughton to arm and outfit his vessel and follow the instructions of the commission, dated September 2, 1775: "You being appointed a Captain in the Army of the United Colonies of North America, are hereby directed to take the command of a detachment of said Army and proceed on board the Schooner *Hanna....*" The commission goes on for ten numbered articles with instructions to board and capture by force enemy vessels, how to treat prisoners of war taken in vessels captured, how the prize money was to be divided, and ends with "be extremely careful and frugal of your ammunition; by no means to waste any of it in salutes or any purpose but what is absolutely necessary."

Captain Broughton's vessel, the *Hanna,* was the first armed vessel in the service of the United States. We can only conjecture how she looked—a Marblehead type of schooner of the size in general use on that coast in 1775, armed with 4 six-pounder guns, manned by a crew of thirty.

The *Hanna* went to sea September 5, and two days later was back in its port of Gloucester. The captain made the welcome report to General Washington: "I sailed from Beverly last Thursday at ten o'clock, saw two ships of war; they gave me chase. I made back towards Cape Ann, but did not go in. Next morning I saw a ship under my lee quarter; she gave me chase, I ran into Cape Ann harbor. I tacked and stood back for the land; soon after I put about and stood towards her again and found her a ship of no force. I came up with her, hailed, and asked where she came from; was answered, from Piscataqua, and bound to Boston. I told him he must bear away and go into Cape Ann; but being very loth, I told him if he did not I should fire on her. On that she bore away and I have brought her safe into Cape Ann harbour, and I have delivered the ship and prisoners into the hands and care of the Committee of Safety for this Town of Gloucester, and have desired them to send the prisoners under proper guard to your Excellency for further orders."

This prize was the ship *Unity,* loaded with a cargo of naval stores. It was the first prize taken by the Continental Navy.

The *Lee* bringing the captured *Nancy* into port

Early in October, 1775, General Washington instructed Colonel Glover of the Marblehead Marines to procure two more vessels at Newbury or Salem and prepare them for armed sea duty with utmost haste. The nation's first war vessel, the *Hanna*, was put aside. The new ones hired were "of better sailing frame." This might have been done as an excuse to ease out the *Hanna*'s mutinous crew, which had embarrassed General Washington.

There was some delay in getting the new vessels, the *Lynch* and the *Franklin*, to sea. Because of the pressing need of gunpowder for the army camped before Boston, four more vessels in addition to these new ones were commissioned. By October 29, ready for sea duty were the *Lynch, Franklin, Lee, Warren, Washington,* and *Harrison*—a small navy which was known as Washington's Cruisers. The ensign proposed by General Washington's secretary, Colonel Reed, was "a flag with a white ground, a tree in the middle, the motto, 'An Appeal to Heaven.' "

These vessels cruised with some success, but General Washington wrote to the President of the Congress: "The plague, trouble and vexation I have had with the crews of all the armed vessels is inexpressible. I believe there is not on earth a more disorderly set."

Just at the time of this letter, good luck struck like lightning. John Manley, a forty-two-year-old mariner who had lived since early manhood at Marblehead, was the captain of the schooner *Lee*. He had learned that two of three British supply vessels that sailed in company had arrived in port and the third was expected. He set out to intercept the third ship.

On November 29 he sighted sail, the object of his search. She was the brigantine *Nancy*, with a large cargo of war matériel —matériel that would have taken the colonial patriots two years to manufacture even if they had had the ways to do it.

The *Lee* brought the *Nancy* into Cape Ann harbor in Massachusetts; the news was sent to General Washington in a report. He, in turn, informed the President of Congress, John Hancock, with a letter from Cambridge dated November 30:

"Last evening I received the agreeable account of the schooner *Lee* Commanded by Captain Manley have taken & carried into Cape Ann a Large Brigantine bound from London to Boston Loaden with Military Stores, the Inventory of which I have the pleasure to inclose you. Cape Ann is a very open Harbour and accessible to large ships, which Made Me immediately send off Colonel Glover and Mr. Palfrey, with orders to raise the Minute Men & Militia of that part of the Country, to have the Cargo Landed without Loss of time, & Guarded up to this Camp, this I hope they will be able to effect, before it is known to the enemy, what Port she is carried into, I sincerely Congratulate you on this very great acquisition, & am Sir & c.

> Go. Washington

"P.S. Manley has also taken a sloop in the ministerial Service & Capt. Adams in the schooner *Warren* has taken a Schooner Laden with Potatoes & Turnips bound to Boston, & carried her into Portsmouth."

Captain Manley was appointed Commodore of the Fleet. Many prizes valuable to the American cause were taken. The *Lee* fought an enemy war vessel; the *Lee* and *Franklin* captured a large brigantine; the *Hancock* fought and took two brigs of size in sight of the enemy; the *Franklin*, under Captain Mugford, captured the ship *Hope* laden with a large cargo of arms and seventy-five tons of gunpowder.

One of the first Continental Navy vessels, the *Providence*

The first American armed vessels commissioned by a public authority were the sloops fitted out by Rhode Island on June 15, 1775. The British frigate *Rose* had made several raids on the coast, and in response to these attacks the sloops were put to sea. They chased and destroyed the tender to the *Rose*. One of them, the *Katy*, under Captain Abraham Whipple, next went to Bermuda to capture gunpowder, and in December seized an enemy vessel in Massachusetts Bay.

When Commodore Hopkins was appointed to command the navy, he went to Philadelphia aboard the *Katy*. The sloop, her officers and crew, were all taken into the Continental Navy; the *Katy* was renamed the *Providence*. She was one of "Hopkins' Fleet" which raided New Providence Island in the West Indies, and when she returned to America, her command was given to Lieutenant John Paul Jones on May 10, 1776.

It is assumed from descriptions that this vessel was about average size for a popular type of craft of that era. The *Providence* resembled a Bermuda Clipper. She was 65 feet long on deck, her beam was 21 feet, and she mounted 12 guns. Captain John Paul Jones said this vessel was the best and had the best crew of the many he commanded. This was high praise indeed, for of all the captains in the regular navy, he commanded the most ships and never lost one; he fought the most battles and never suffered defeat, sailed the most miles, and captured the most prizes.

His first orders upon receiving command of the *Providence* were to take army troops by ship from Providence, Rhode Island, to New York and then to return. This was a very dangerous duty just at that time, since the coast was alive with British ships preparing for the invasion of New York. He saw many of the enemy ships but was able to avoid them. Since he was successful in this first assignment, he was ordered to repeat it four times, mostly to convoy other ships. On one cruise Captain Jones saved the brig *Hispaniola* (later to become the American privateer *Hampden*). The

Hispaniola was laden with military stores when she was chased by H.B.M. *Cerberus*. Jones saved her by coming between the large warship and the brig, then outsailing the enemy. He sailed from the Delaware on August 21, and in the latitude of Bermuda fell in with the Royal Navy frigate *Solebay*, 28 guns. The *Providence* so outsailed her that Jones and his crew just toyed with the British ship, making her waste her ammunition. Another enemy frigate, the *Milford*, was treated to the same game. The *Providence* destroyed the English fishing at Canso and Madame Island, Nova Scotia. On October 3, 1776, she was back at Newport harbor, bringing in eight prize vessels of sixteen captured—the other eight were burned. At this time Lieutenant Jones was given command of the flagship *Alfred*.

The *Providence* sailed on and on—cruising, taking prizes, and performing convoy duty. Captain John Rathman, newly appointed to her command, sailed from Georgetown, South Carolina, with a fifty-man crew and made a daring raid on New Providence Island. Both forts there were taken, and the entire island was in the hands of the crew for four days. They returned home with thirty-two Americans who had been prisoners, 1,600 pounds of gunpowder, a supply of muskets, provisions, and five vessels taken in the harbor. About six weeks later Captain Rathman took five prizes, all brought safely to port. After several more cruises, Captain Rathman took command of a frigate, and Captain Hacker became master of the *Providence*.

On May 7, 1779, while cruising off Sandy Hook peninsula, New Jersey, at nine in the morning, the *Providence* saw the British brig *Diligent*. About noon the two vessels closed for action. The enemy was cut to pieces, and with all of the crew and officers wounded, she was brought back to port and taken into the Continental Navy. The *Providence* was one of the Continental Navy vessels that was lost on the expedition by the State of Massachusetts to capture Penobscot Bay and River from the British in 1779.

John Paul Jones on the *Alfred* first raised the United States flag

"I hoisted with my own hands the Flag of Freedom the first time it was displayed, on the *Alfred*, on the Delaware...." John Paul Jones wrote on December 7, 1779, in a letter to the President of the Continental Congress, John Hancock. The event described took place when this naval hero was first appointed senior lieutenant on the Continental Navy flagship *Alfred*. He did not give the date of this occurrence. It has been established as December 3, 1775, from the report of a Loyalist informer to the Earl of Dartmouth, in a letter of December 20, 1775: "An admiral is appointed, a court established, and the 3ᵈ instant, the Continental flag on board the *Black Prince* opposite Philadelphia was hoisted." (The *Black Prince* had been renamed the *Alfred*.)

This would have been the Grand Union flag, respected as the first flag of the United States—the one that flew over General Washington's headquarters at New York when the Declaration of Independence was read to the troops. For the first years of the American Revolution, the Grand Union was the nation's flag on land and sea.

How the flag came to be designed can only be surmised. At that time, the British naval flag in use on American waters was the "White"—a white field with the Union Jack employed as a canton. It would seem that the patriot founders of the United States, who wanted a flag of their own and at the same time clung to their mother country, added to the British naval flag a differentiating mark: the thirteen stripes. Some hold that this flag originated in the colonial navy.

Naval flags of those days were enormous by later standards. It was the fashion to display very large ensigns at the sterns of war-ships, and marine paintings of the time give evidence of this. There was a feeling left over from more than two centuries of naval warfare that a great banner betokened the might of the nation behind it.

No more honorable place could have been found to display this first flag than from the staff of the Continental Navy flagship *Alfred*, because all who made the young nation's affairs their own in 1775 looked on this ship and the fleet she headed as the representatives of freedom and liberty, and the defenders of their homes. Letters from the patriot citizens show their enthusiasm for their navy.

The *Alfred* had been the successful Philadelphia-built packet, the *Black Prince*. Captain John Barry was her master on several trade cargo crossings. The Marine Committee purchased and converted her to a warship. She carried 24 guns, reduced from 30. Her appearance is described in a British Intelligence Service dispatch of January 4, 1776: "This day about one o'clock sailed the *Alfred* and the ship, *Columbus*, with two brigs.... Hopkins commands the *Alfred*. She has yellow sides, her head the figure of a man."

The career of this ship was admirable indeed. After her first cruises, her command was given to Lieutenant John Paul Jones. She stung the enemy more than once. On a six weeks' cruise she returned with six prizes, and many times she outsailed and escaped from large Royal Navy men-of-war.

In the painting, the other vessels shown with their flagship were the first in the United States Navy to be called *Hornet* (a sloop) and *Wasp* (a schooner).

The first Continental Navy force, Commodore Hopkins' fleet

The first Continental Navy task force made rendezvous at Cape Henlopen, near Delaware Bay, on February 17, 1776, and from there the ships sailed to make a descent on New Providence Island, in the West Indies. Left to right in the painting are: the brig *Cabot,* 14 guns; the brig *Andrea Doria,* 14 guns; the flagship *Alfred,* 24 guns; the sloop *Hornet,* 10 guns; the frigate tender *Fly*; the ship *Columbus,* 20 guns; the sloop *Providence,* 12 guns; and the schooner *Wasp,* 8 guns.

Some of these honored names have been used over and over in the United States naval service, but they originated with the Marine Committee of the Continental Congress. John Adams, as a member of the committee, wrote: "The first we named *Alfred* in honor of the founder of the greatest Navy that ever existed. The second *Columbus* after the Discoverer of this quarter of the Globe. The third *Cabot,* for the Discoverer of this northern Part of the Continent. The forth, *Andrea Doria,* in memory of the Greatest Genoese Admiral and the fifth, *Providence,* for the town where she was purchased, the residence of Governor Hopkins and his Brother Esek whom we appointed first Captain."

The *Alfred* had been the *Black Prince*; the *Columbus* had been the *Sally.* The former names of the *Cabot* and *Andrea Doria* are not known for certain. The *Providence* was the sloop *Katy.* (Captain Whipple brought her and the crew from Rhode Island.) The *Hornet, Fly,* and *Wasp* were Baltimore vessels, each with her own crew which joined the others two days before sailing. Commodore Esek Hopkins, in command, held the naval rank equal to General Washington's rank as Commander in Chief.

The only officer in the fleet with first-rate naval experience was twenty-six-year-old Captain Nicholas Biddle, in command of the *Andrea Doria*: He had been a midshipman in the Royal Navy. The most experienced mariner may have been twenty-nine-year-old John Paul Jones.

There was a rumor that New Providence Island was heavily stocked with arms and gunpowder for the British to use on the rebelling American colonies, so without any particular orders from Congress, Commodore Hopkins determined to raid that stronghold, though ice in the Delaware held the fleet back for some time. A "Gale of Wind" separated some of the ships, but they all had assembled at Abaco, in the Bahamas, by March, 1776. Hopkins, in his report, said: "I put in Execution the 3rd March by Landing 200 Marines under the Command of Captn. Nicholas and 50 Sailors under the command of Lieutt. Weaver. . . ."

For beginners at warfare, this duty was handsomely performed. It took Captain Nicholas an afternoon and the following morning to gain complete possession of the forts and command of the island. In this first combat, the American Marines behaved with the spirit and steadiness that have distinguished the Corps ever since. After holding the island for a few days, the fleet left on March 17, taking away the governor and some of his men.

The quantity of arms was not as great as expected; nevertheless, over 100 cannon and large amounts of other stores fell to the Americans. The ships returned safely to American ports. This was the only action of these vessels as a squadron, and it proved that the new nation was not helpless at sea.

The Continental Navy *Lexington* taking the H.M.S. *Edward*

One of the best deals that the Marine Committee made for the Continental Congress must have been the buying of the *Wild Duck*. She was a brig; a bit more than 90 feet from her beak to her transom top. She had a 24-foot, 6-inch beam; her sides were pierced for 14 four-pounder guns, and she also had 12 swivels. In Philadelphia she was remodeled into a warship by the famous shipbuilder Joshua Humphreys. He sent his bill April 1, 1776, "for outfitting the Continental brig *Lexington*." That was her new name.

Captain John Barry had followed the sea all his life. He was master of the *Black Prince* when she was purchased for the navy as the *Alfred*. He offered his services to his country and was given the command of the Continental Navy brig *Lexington*.

It was a gloomy, rainy Sunday—rain all the way from Boston to Charleston, South Carolina—when the following report was made:

"In sight of the Virginia Capes April 7, 1776. Gentlemen: I have the pleasure to acquaint you, that at one P.M. this day I fell in with the sloop *Edward*, belonging to the *Liverpool* frigate. She engaged us near two hours. We shattered her in a terrible manner as you will see. We killed and wounded several of her crew. I shall give you a particular account of the powder and arms taken out of her, as well as my proceedings in general. I have the pleasure to acquaint you that all our people behaved with much courage. I am, gentlemen

John Barry"

The *Lexington* got her prize, the *Edward*, safely to Philadelphia. After her own rather extensive war damage had been repaired, she went out again convoying ships on the coast.

Captain Hammon, of the H.M.S. *Roebuck*, was the master of the group of several enemy ships patrolling the Delaware. In his report to his admiral, he sounded rather exasperated in saying that the "rebel brig" [*Lexington*] kept just out of his gun range, and that when his ships started to chase her, she would navigate close to the coast where the water was not deep enough for him to follow.

On June 29, 1776, the armed brig *Nancy*, from the West Indies, was bound for Philadelphia with military stores for General Washington's army. Off Cape May she was chased by six British war vessels. It was the afternoon of a dark day and she was managing to resist the enemy when the *Reprisal* and *Lexington* came to her rescue. They held the enemy off while the *Nancy* purposely ran onto the shore, placed her guns so as to make a fort of the place, and with the help of the ships kept the enemy at bay until the crew could get the arms and 274 barrels of powder into the hands of the local citizens who had come running to help when they heard the firing.

Captain Barry took command of the new "a-building" frigate *Effingham,* and the *Lexington,* under a new captain, went on a cruise to the West Indies. On returning, and while off the Delaware capes she was captured by H.M.S. *Pearl*, and a British prize crew—a lieutenant and five men—were put in charge of the *Lexington* with her crew of seventy men. That evening the prisoners retook their ship and got her back to Philadelphia without the aid of officers to command them.

Now, the ship, restored to life and sparkle, came under the command of Captain Henry Johnson. He sailed her from Baltimore on February 27, 1777, bound for France, arriving April 1. It was then that the *Lexington* teamed up with the *Reprisal* and *Dolphin* to take the war to the coast of England.

The South Carolina Navy in "Rebellion Row"

By June of 1775, all of the North American colonies were alive to the fact that the mother country was taking stern measures against their coastal shipping and commerce and especially against their trade in the West Indies.

The Assembly of Rhode Island, on August 26, 1775, declared: "the building and equiping of an American fleet would greatly and essentially conduce the preservation of the lives, liberty and prosperity of the good people of these colonies." And forthwith they fitted out two vessels to protect their coasts. One of them was the *Providence.*

Ten of the other colonies rushed with Rhode Island to form state navies which varied both in the number and the size of the vessels. Massachusetts, Pennsylvania, and South Carolina had the largest numbers of ships and crew members. Georgia, smallest in population and far away from the newly raised government, contributed a schooner and five galleys. These state navies were maintained throughout the war.

South Carolina did not have a shipbuilding coast. During all her life as a settlement, ships of the world had called at her ports for the products of her fields and swamps. Because of the sudden need to defend her shores, the Council of Safety purchased ships wherever they could be found. A South Carolina sloop that had been armed and sent out captured a British warship off the coast of Florida in August, 1775. Also, South Carolina had the colonial schooners *Defence* and *Comet* fitted out and armed.

On Sundy morning, November 12, 1775, the *Defence,* under Captain Tuffs, was guarding and aiding in the war measure of sinking four hulks in the channel of Hog Island Creek. The king's warship *Tamer,* 16 guns, and *Cherokee,* 6 guns, came up abeam to fire broadside at the *Defence.*

The fire was returned and kept up until the work was finished. There was damage and injury on both sides. However, when the enemy was fired on, he seemed timid about retaliating. In the city of Charleston, drums beat to arms, the militia assembled under their officers, and the citizens were alerted. At this time there was a fine new ship just arrived in Charleston harbor, the *Prosper* from Bristol. That night, at an extraordinary meeting of the Congress and Council of Safety, a bill was passed: "Resolved—that the ship *Prosper* be immediately impressed and taken into the service of the Colony, fitted and armed as a frigate of war with utmost expedition."

A fair value was placed on the ship, and her master was asked to accept payment for her for the owners, but he declined. He was given transportation money back to England and sent to the West Indies where he could find passage.

The *Prosper, Defence,* and *Comet,* under Commodore Gabriel Powell, went out to guard the Charleston harbor roadsteads later to be known by the South Carolina patriots as Rebellion Row.

This state was to have a considerable force in her navy—fifteen ships of size, and several equal to regular navy frigates. In much the same way, other state navy forces came into being.

The British driven from the Delaware River

The Philadelphia Committee of Safety, in order to defend their city from the side which faced the river, had an obstruction placed in the river. This was a *cheval-de-frise,* made of sharp-ended logs which stuck up at an angle below the waterline, and would block any invasion by ships. They also assembled a flotilla of vessels about the city—a 10-gun battery; a barge with 24 large guns; 13 gondolas, each with an 18- or 24-pounder; and fireboats and rafts loaded with hay and combustibles.

There was truth in the rumor that the two enemy warships, H.M.S. *Roebuck,* 44 guns and *Liverpool,* 28 guns, were to come up the river to do any damage they could. Captain Hammond of the *Roebuck,* when he received orders from his admiral "to patrol the river as far as the city and interrupt all water commerce," replied that he would attempt to obey orders and do his utmost to execute them. It was his opinion, however, based on reports from informers, that the river had become rather formidable and a much larger force than his two ships would be needed.

Despite his apprehension of the hazards, he headed the two warships up the river, and on May 8, 1776—a beautiful spring day with a gentle breeze, just enough to fill the sails of the big ships—was below the city.

The two lookouts along the riverbanks were not slow in getting word back to the Philadelphia Committee of Safety, and the flotilla which had been ready started down to fight the British.

Words left behind from that day tell of the events: ". . . near 2 went to the Coffee house the city alarmed with hearing great number of heavy cannon firing down river, the Drums beat to arms & number of volunteers went down in boats in order to assist as the report was that the Roe Buck of 40 & the Liverpole of 28 guns with tenders were got above New Castle standing up the river." (From Christopher Marshall's diary)

"Wilmington
Wednesday 8th May 1776

Gentlemen:

Our boats and the two men of war have been ingaged for two hours at long shot. I believe there is no danger done on either side, tho' I suppose three or four hundred shot have passed between them, the men of war are the Roebuck of 48 guns & the Liverpool of 28. Our Boats fire much better than the other Vessels but in my oppinion ingage at too great a distance. The *Wasp* being at Wilmington as soon as the men of war had past the creek's mouth, sail'd out and has taken a brig which he is now bringing in. I wrote this from the Bank of the river where I have been with one hundred Riflemen ever since morning in order to afford any assistance that might be wanted. A great deal of ammunition has been wasted. I am tho' cold & hungary, Gentlemen &

Sam Miles."

This letter was to the Committee of Safety. The *Wasp* mentioned in the letter was the Continental Navy schooner, 8 guns. She captured the tender to the *Liverpool,* the sloop *Betsey,* and hurried her down the river, hiding out from the British ships. They looked for their sloop, but never did find her, and the *Betsey* ended up in the Continental Navy.

Captain Hammond told some Tory friends at a later date that if the commanders of the galleys had acted with as much judgment as they had courage, they would have taken or destroyed his ship. Most of the Philadelphia watermen on the flotilla craft worked a gun for the first time. Philadelphia was not attacked from the river until October, 1777.

The Virginia State Navy *Cruizer* taking the H.M.S. *Oxford*

From Newport, on May 19, 1776, the Continental Navy brigs *Andrea Doria* and *Cabot* went in company on a cruise eastward to search for prizes as well as to spy on the number of troop transports reported bound from England to Halifax. They had been at sea for just a few days when they were chased by H.M.S. *Cerberus* and separated.

On May 29, in latitude 41° 19′ N, longitude 57° 12′ W, the *Andrea Doria* captured two transport vessels and noted the event in her journal: "At 4 A.M. saw two ships to ye North'd, Made Sail and Hauld our Wind to ye North'd. At 6 Do. Brought the Northermost too, as ship from Glascow with 100 Highland Troops on Board & officers; made her hoist her Boat out & the Capt. came on board. Detained the Boat till we Brought the other too, from Gloscow with ye same number of troops. Lieutenant James Josiah went on board and sent ye Capt. and four Men on board ye Brig, received orders for sending all the troops on board the other ship and went Prize master with Eleven Hands. Sent all the arms on board ye Brig *Andrea Doria* from both ships, two hundred & odd."

These transport vessels were the *Oxford* and the *Crawford*. All of the 217 soldiers, several women, and children were put on board the *Oxford*.

The *Andrea Doria* cruised with her prizes for two weeks, attempting to avoid British ships and get back to port. Off Nantucket Shoals they were chased by five British vessels. Captain Biddle of the *Andrea Doria* signaled to the transports to steer different courses and lost sight of them while escaping from the enemy.

On board the *Oxford* the British soldiers overcame the prize crew and took possession of the vessel, setting her course southward.

Not long thereafter, at just about daylight, a Virginia Navy vessel commanded by Captain James Barron sighted a sail to the east. After ranging up to the stranger and seeing her British colors, he ran up his vessel's flag and opened fire with a broadside. The exchange of shot was hot and rapid; that from the enemy was well directed. Captain Barron could see that the enemy vessel was loaded with soldiers and from the maneuvering she was doing, was making an attempt to close with his vessel to board. His crew, less than seventy, would have no chance against so many. He loaded his guns with chain shot. The first round cut the British ship's mainmast asunder and chewed up her rigging so badly that she was almost helpless. The Britisher was the *Oxford* and the Virginia Navy vessel circled about her firing at her bow and stern until her crew hauled down her colors in surrender.

Captain Barron ordered the *Oxford* to send her boat to his vessel with her master. Aboard the Virginia Navy vessel came the *Oxford*'s mate who was acting as her captain and two officers of the troops. Terms of surrender were agreed on and the enemy transport, loaded with British soldiers, was taken as a prize into Jamestown, Virginia, in June, 1776.

The name of this Virginia Navy vessel is not known with any exactness. Some accounts call her the *Cruizer* and others refer to her as the *Liberty* or the *Adventurer*. It is also not known whether she was a brig or a sloop—but Captain Barron had his hands full in capturing the *Oxford* with her 200 angry enemy soldiers, when his crew numbered less than seventy men.

The *Crawford* was recaptured by H.M.S. *Cerberus*, and Lieutenant Josiah, the prize master, was treated brutally. Later the *Crawford* was captured again by the American ship *General Schuyler* and taken into Newport.

The Battle of Lake Champlain

All phases of the Battle of Lake Champlain are replete with tales of daring and bravery, from the Battle of Valcour Bay on October 11, 1776, to the last hours of fighting two days later at noon. Here is General Benedict Arnold's narrative of the running fight:

"The *Washington* galley was in such a shattered condition and had so many men killed and wounded, she struck to the enemy after receiving a few broadsides. We were then attacked in the *Congress* galley by a ship mounting eighteen twelve pounders, a schooner of fourteen sixes and one of twelve sixes, two under our stern and one on our broadsides within musket shot. They kept up an incessant fire on us for about five glasses with round and grape shot, which we returned as briskly. The sails, rigging and hull of the *Congress* were shattered and torn in pieces, the First Lieutenant and three men killed, when to prevent her falling into the enemy's hands, who had seven sail around me, I ran her ashore in a small creek ten miles from Crown Point on the east side; when after saving our small arms, I set her on fire with four gondolas, with whose crews I reached Crown Point through the woods that evening and very luckily escaped the savages [Indians in the pay of the British] who waylaid the road in two hours after we passed."

The Americans had lost the lake, but now another foe faced the British—winter. They withdrew from the lake to await springtime, and this gap in the fighting is credited by historians as the one most important thing that saved General Washington's army. The delaying action by General Arnold's little American naval force gave the army time to rally to defeat General Burgoyne's troops thrown against them in 1777.

The Congress had given General Arnold the command to defend the lake in July, 1776. He at once started buying and building vessels that could be armed, and those built under his directions are some of the most interesting of all naval history. Three of them were General Arnold's flagships *Congress, Trumbull,* and *Washington*. Their length was 75 feet, beam 20 feet; they drew 7 feet of water; each had 10 guns.

The *Washington* was captured by the British, remodeled, and used on the lake for years. It is from British drawings of her that it is known how these vessels looked. The gondolas were about 53 feet long, beam 16 feet flat-bottomed. According to their builders, Vermont woodsmen, they were "made to sail only north and south" (up and down the lake). One was raised from the lake bottom and can still be seen in the Smithsonian Institution.

General Arnold had sixteen major vessels when the fighting started. He opposed the British, who had a complete navy. The largest enemy ship was a seagoing vessel that had been taken apart at Quebec, carried overland part by part, and reassembled on the lake at St. John's. The British had spent a year putting together their navy—five large vessels, twenty gunboats, four longboats, and twenty-four boats loaded with stores and provisions. Their guns numbered twice those of the Americans.

All this was 200 years ago. An American who was there said of the closing moments on board the flagship *Congress:* "General Arnold fought like a lion."

The Continental Navy *Andrea Doria* under easy sail

How many out of one hundred American people in 1776 could read and write may not be known, but it is safe to assume that the percentage that could not read was higher among the seafaring people than almost any other group. This was the case in England, and at that time the pattern in America was almost the same. For the Marine Committee and for Patriots such as John Adams who knew history, the name of the Continental Navy brig *Andrea Doria* might have been easily read and pronounced, but for many of the men who sailed on her that name was a complete puzzle. They called her *Andrew Doria, Andy Dora,* and *Aunt Dora.* Even the more learned had some trouble with her name. A British Intelligence report of January 4, 1776, lists her as *Annodoria.*

Few indeed seemed to know that she was named for the George Washington of another day and place, the father and liberator of his country, Prince of Melfi—Knight of the Order of the Golden Fleece—Admiral Andrea Doria of Genoa, Italy. At one time he commanded 500 ships. In various parts of the world, for 200 years "Andrea Doria" meant "power on the sea," and to this day it is a great name to the people of the Mediterranean.

What the name of the *Andrea Doria* was before she was purchased for the Continental Navy is not clearly known; a record says it was *Defence,* or that could have been an interim name until *Andrea Doria* was selected. Nor is it known where she was built or when. She was fitted out for naval service with 14 guns and a crew of 130—about the same size as the *Lexington* and the *Cabot,* or perhaps a bit larger. To convert her to a war vessel, Joshua Humphreys, the contractor at

Philadelphia, had more than thirty men—mostly carpenters—at work on her. He sent his bill on December 30, 1775.

Captain Nicholas Biddle was her first commander, and as the best-trained and most experienced naval officer, even at the age of twenty-six, in the Continental Navy, his judgment of the qualities of the vessel can be accepted when he stated that the *Andrea Doria* was the best, and could outsail all others in Hopkins' fleet.

The *Andrea Doria* dropped down the Delaware River from Philadelphia to join Commodore Hopkins' fleet at Reedy Island on January 17, 1776, to make up one of the task force squadron for a raid on New Providence Island. From there they went to Cape Henlopen, where, while waiting to get started, Captain Biddle wrote to his brother: . . . "I now muster 109 Men in the Whole, am in every Respect well equipt. I have by great odds the fastest sailing Vessel in the fleet. . . ."

The sailing of this fleet was carried in many colonial newspapers. In *Dixon & Hunters' Virginia Gazette* of March 2, 1776, we read: "By a Gentleman from Philadelphia, we have received the pleasing account of actual sailing from that place of the first American fleet that ever swelled their sails on the Western ocean in defence of the rights and liberties of the people of these colonies, now suffering under the persecuting rod of the British Ministry, and their more than brutish tyrants in America. This fleet consists of five sail, fitted out at Philadelphia, which are to be joined at the Capes of Virginia by two ships from Maryland. . . ." The article goes on to name the ships, getting the name of the *Andrea Doria* wrong.

Launching the Continental Navy frigate *Randolph*

One of the most important dates in United States naval history is December 13, 1775, the day that the Continental Congress resolved to establish a navy and provide ships. Part of the journal of that day reads:

"The Committee appointed to devise ways and means for fitting out naval armament, brought in their report, which being taken into consideration was agreed to as follows:

"That five ships of thirty-two guns, five of twenty-eight guns, three of twenty-four guns, making in the whole thirteen, can be fitted for the sea probily [*sic*] by the last of March next, viz. in New Hampshire one, in Massachusetts Bay two, in Rhode Island two, in Connecticut one, in New York two, in Pensylvania [*sic*] four and in Maryland one.

"The cost of these ships so fitted out will be not more than 66,666 ⅔ dollars each, on an average, allowing two complete suits of sails for each ship, equal in the whole to 866,666 ⅔ dollars."

From the time this second Continental Congress assembled, almost a fourth of the debate time had been about naval matters. John Adams greatly favored having a navy, and in his diary reported that Mr. Chase, delegate from Maryland, declared, "It is the maddest idea in the world to think of building an American fleet; we should mortgage the whole continent." A number of the delegates agreed with Mr. Chase, but not a majority; they followed the persuasive speech of Mr. Wythe of Virginia. He reminded them that Rome did not have a navy, and when she faced the fact that she had to fight on the sea, in a year's time she built, equipped, and manned a fleet that defeated the masters of the sea—Carthage—and that the United States could do the same.

The committee that allocated when and how many vessels each shipbuilding center was to have knew its work very well. There was little political favoritism, for to have these ships was a most serious matter for all the colonial Patriots. The long Atlantic coastline and the ocean washing its shores was their one and only link with the world beyond. Their lives were daily touched and stirred by the sea and ships. Never was a Congress more closely in touch with its people than in 1775 and 1776, when it enacted the Navy Bill.

The Continental Navy frigate *Randolph,* 32 guns, one of the original thirteen ships and one of Pennsylvania's four, was built by Wharton and Humphreys, an established and experienced firm. The plan ("draught") of this frigate is still to be seen in the nation's archives—a very professional drawing—by whose hand it is not known.

Prior to 1776 there had been only one warship built in North America and that was when the men of 1776 were small boys and only a few ships that were as heavy and large had ever been built on these shores. Therefore, any shipbuilder receiving a contract to build a frigate would first need to lay out new ways or enlarge present ones. The shipyards of Europe and England had ways and docks built of stone, large works that could handle a 100-gun ship. They had equipment for hoisting, workboats especially fitted out to set masts, and mast houses—tall buildings in which masts were stored on end. But in 1776 America had one thing that Europe did not have: timber—miles after miles of forest. The American colonists were the world's experts at cutting, sawing, and using timber, and their shipyards made full use of the talents in their new undertaking.

Building the frigate *Montgomery* on the Hudson River

Perhaps it caused no astonishment at all in 1776 to be riding through the green and pleasant Hudson River valley at Poughkeepsie, New York, and to come upon two large warships under construction. That is where the two frigates allocated to New York were built by Lancaster Burling: the *Congress,* 32 guns, and the *Montgomery,* 24 guns.

The Marine Committee took its duty with utmost seriousness and the contracts they awarded for their ships were placed only in the hands of experienced and worthy builders. Fine Hudson River craft had been built in the Poughkeepsie locality for many years. Nothing the size of a frigate had been constructed there, but then that was true of all the shipyards in America.

Until the last of the eighteenth century, the art of shipbuilding was a secret trade, known only to master shipbuilders and those who worked under them. The secrets were how to determine the scantlings (how large to make the timbers) and how to lay out the patterns, on a molding floor or in a loft, for the compound shapes and curves. The master shipbuilder was usually a very practical man with ships. For constructing these men-of-war, the builder selected as a site a gently sloping bank where the 200-foot ways could be laid down. It would need good depth, perhaps at the bend of a river, for launching the hull.

Near the inland, sheltered shipyard of Poughkeepsie was timber which could be used for the sleepers and blocks, scaffolding and ramps. Oak for the hulls could be floated down the river. The work of the shipyard was almost 99 percent work with wood, for metal for the shipbuilders of the American Revolution was in very short supply. The shipwright—a different trade from the ship carpenter—executed the metalwork. He had to do with making and stepping (standing up) the masts.

To build a ship was hard work, from sunup to sunset. To move the heavy timbers, mule teams and oxen, blocks and tackle, and "timber carriages"—large two-wheeled devices with an arch axle to lift and carry a log—were used. A gang of men was required to lift complexly cut timber, carry it up a ramp, and hold it in place until its fastener was driven home. The tools that a ship carpenter used were heavier and not at all the same as those a home or barn builder used. The sound of the turning grindstone was heard all day, for the cutting edge of the ship carpenter's tools had to be extremely sharp indeed.

The sawing of lumber was unending. Planks were cut from logs on saw frames over sawpits. A young, strong man pulled the saw from his position in the pit. He lived in a constant shower of sawdust coming down on his head, and his wages were less than those of the older man on top of the log who guided the saw. The hard physical labor and skilled craft that went into the work of warship building in the days of sail are today beyond belief.

The *Congress* and *Montgomery* were launched and partly fitted out. But after the Battle of Long Island the British held the lower Hudson River; there was no way to get these frigates to the sea. They were burned about ten miles down the river from where they were built—burned by the men who built them.

The Continental Navy frigate *Virginia* on the stocks

The only contemporaneous painting of an American shipyard of the eighteenth century is one near Baltimore. The part of the Chesapeake Bay near Baltimore had for many years been a shipbuilding center, the home of the Baltimore Clipper. The Marine Committee awarded the contract to build the warship allocated to Maryland to George Wells of that city. She was the Continental Navy frigate *Virginia*, 28 guns. Her length from figurehead to taffrail was 148 feet; her beam 34 feet 4 inches. On the ways, the distance from her keel to her quarterdeck rail at the highest point was 34 feet 4 inches. Scaffolding at the stern of this ship was 40 feet above the ground. Her plan and many of her features were much the same as the *Randolph*, except that the *Virginia* was a smaller ship by a few feet.

The hulls of all the Continental Navy frigates presented a problem. England and France had the money to put copper plates on the parts of their ships' hulls below the waterline. The United States had neither copper nor the money to buy it. Prior to the American Revolution the old system was to coat this part of a hull with pitch, sulfur, hair, and feathers, covered over with a light wood sheathing. All of this was to prevent sea worms from boring holes into the wooden hulls. This system by 1776 had about been given up as not effective. It seems that the Continental Navy frigates had only fine crude oil from Pennsylvania mixed with pitch to coat their hulls. In seawater this mixture hardened and was a fair coating to protect the wood.

There was some difficulty getting the *Virginia* launched—always the critical part of shipbuilding. She was started early in 1776, but it was a full year before she was ready for sea duty.

The Congress appointed Captain James Nicholson to be her commander, and in April his superiors ordered him to sea to cruise to the West Indies. Because of the tight British blockade of the Chesapeake, however, the *Virginia* was kept in port. Repeated orders were issued, but were not followed for the same reason. The ship remained idle in port all year.

It was March 30, 1778, before it looked like she had a chance to ship out—it was rumored that the enemy had relaxed their blockade. The waters of the upper part of the Chesapeake were then full of bars and shoals and difficult to navigate. Captain Nicholson was to follow a brig down the bay, the pilot of the brig being considered an expert on navigating these waters.

The *Virginia* cast her moorings at noon and proceeded to follow the brig; a stern lantern guided her at night. At three o'clock in the morning she grounded heavily in shoal water, and as the tide went out she tilted on her starboard side, opening up some of her seams and causing her to leak rather badly. Also, her rudder had been forced back, springing all the pins.

At daylight two sails were seen coming up the bay until they got within pistol range: the British men-of-war H.B.M. *Emerald* and *Conquerer*. There was nothing the helpless *Virginia* could do but surrender. The Englishmen refloated her and took her to England where her "lines were taken off" (*i.e.*, she was put in drydock and measured for a working drawing). She was sold in 1786.

The *Surprise* taking the British mail packet the *Prince of Orange*

William Hodge, a Philadelphia merchant, was sent to France with Congressional dispatches to the American commissioners at Paris. As he was known to them as a reliable ship broker, they employed him to buy vessels for the Continental Navy service. He proceeded to Dunkirk, where in April, 1777, he obtained a large lugger.

This type of vessel was used by the French—seldom by the English—and therefore was not favored by the American seamen. Luggers were suited to the Mediterranean. Their simple sail and rigging made them easy to handle with a small crew, but they were hardly rugged enough for the Atlantic waters. The one that Hodge bought, named *Surprise,* was rigged for the French Atlantic coast.

In Dunkirk Hodge came upon another Philadelphian, Gustavus Conyngham, a sea captain, who was in Europe to procure military supplies for his country. Hodge recommended this captain to the commissioners as an able man to take command of the *Surprise.* Accordingly, the commissioners filled out for him one of the blank "captain's papers" that the Congress had authorized them to use. The date was March 1, 1777.

If they had searched the world over they could not have put this commission into more able hands, for Captain Conyngham was one of those who by nature seem to be part man, part ship, part seawater. He was to become one of America's five greatest commanders in her first war.

Ten brass cannon barrels were found at Dunkirk, and a couple of swivels to fit out the *Surprise.* She was ready for sea about May 1. She slipped away one foggy morning. Her crew was made up of Americans and Frenchmen. In just a few days she was back at Dunkirk with two fat prizes—one of them the mail packet *Prince of Orange* from Harwich, England, taken without firing a single shot.

The British ambassador to France, Lord Stormont, raised such a protest over these prizes being received in a French port that France's minister of foreign affairs, Vergennes, was obliged to make a drastic move. The *Surprise* was seized, her prizes were released to the English, and Captain Conyngham and his crew thrown into prison. On this occasion the captain's commission papers were taken from him, and to this day have not been found—a matter that was to cause him great hardship.

Lord Stormont recorded with satisfaction: "The success of my application with regard to the Dunkirk Pirate has been highly displeasing to Franklin and Dean" (the American commissioners). But Vergennes notified the French ambassador in London that the prizes had been restored to the English, "not for love of them but only to do homage to the principles of justice and equity."

When word that the American captain and his crew were in prison reached Benjamin Franklin in Paris, he at once procured an order for their release. Captain Conyngham from prison asked that the order not be executed at once because it was no easy matter to find such a crew as he had on the *Surprise,* and prison would be a good place to keep them together until the commissioners had another ship ready for them.

The cutter *Revenge* capturing a British merchantman

A first-class English cutter was up for sale at Dunkirk, and William Hodge purchased her for the Continental Navy by order of the American commissioners. She did not require much work to fit her out, and was kept from public view. Nevertheless, the British ambassador to France, Lord Stormont, through his agents, had been kept fully informed about the cutter. His remonstrances to the French minister were extremely earnest, and put forth to represent that allowing the Americans to have this vessel would put relations between France and England in jeopardy. Therefore, some way had to be arranged to smooth over this affair.

Hodge, a master entrepreneur, found an Englishman in Dunkirk who showed papers—fictions—that it was he who had bought the cutter and swore that she was to go to the Baltic in the timber trade. The British ambassador, who was no fool, was suspicious of the entire thing but had no ready answer, so he dropped the matter.

Captain Conyngham had been given new commission papers, dated May 2, 1777, to replace those taken from him when he was imprisoned. They read in part: "Not to attack but if attacked at Liberty to retaliate in every manner in our power—Burn, Sink & Destroy the enemy."

He had been kept in the know about the new cutter, had directed outfitting her from prison, and when she was ready, fully commissioned, and supplied with provisions, the doors of Dunkirk Prison opened and he marched his crew of 106 men, including sixty-six Frenchmen, aboard their new ship, the Continental Navy cutter *Revenge,* 14 guns. The moorings were cast off at once without any ceremony, and they were out to sea. A London paper reported that its crew was "composed of all the most desperate fellows which could be procured in so blessed a port as Dunkirk."

On the day after sailing, the captain wrote, "was fired on, attacked, chased by several british frigotts [*sic*], sloops of War and Cutters." But the *Revenge* had escaped the waiting British to cruise the North Sea, the Irish Sea, and the Bay of Biscay, sending many prizes to Spanish ports.

The Spanish people were generally friendly to the American cause and treated with hospitality the vessels of the new nation when they visited her ports. The *Revenge* made Bilbao her home when in need of water, supplies, and refit work.

The capture of the British brig *Panoma,* 16 guns, off Portugal, is typical of the more than seventy vessels fought and taken, and sent to port or burned. Captain Conyngham and his vessel became so troublesome to the English who traded with Portugal that orders were issued to the Royal Navy to "follow him into any port and destroy him."

In December, 1778, the *Revenge* cruised for six weeks out of Martinique, taking a number of prizes. At one time it fought and beat off a 24-gun British cutter.

The *Revenge* went into Philadelphia on February 21, 1779, and for reasons never made clear, was sold out of the navy. With Captain Conyngham still in command, she was fitted out as an American privateer. In April she was captured by the H.M.S. *Galatea* and taken to New York. The captain was sent to England in irons and treated with the greatest severity. He was accused of piracy on the grounds that his cruise in the *Surprise* in the spring of 1777 predated his captain's commission. His first papers would have disproved this charge. Confined to Mill Prison, he nevertheless managed to make his escape across England to Holland and joined John Paul Jones on the frigate *Alliance.*

The American privateer *Montgomery* taking the *Millern*

The British Navy had fifty of her 270 ships in North America on December 1, 1775. This was almost as many as the total the British had in home port and on guardship duty, and far more than they had on any other station. When Britain started transporting troops to America in 1776 for the invasion of New York, there were so few of her warships left in her own waters that it was safer for American privateers to cruise on English waters than off their own coast. Later the British force was enlarged.

It was at this time that Dr. Franklin wrote: "We continue to insult the coasts of the Lords of the Ocean with our little cruizers."

Two of these little cruisers were the *Rover* and the *Montgomery* of Philadelphia, the latter a brig of 18 guns. They went to English waters in company and took prizes, which they sent back to America.

Operating so far from home, they had to fill their water casks and obtain stores on the enemy coast. When they visited Galway, a letter relates: "Two American privateers put in here to procure some fresh provisions and water. On being supplied with such necessaries as they wanted, for which they paid in dollars, they weighed anchor and sailed after being in the bay only twenty-four hours. During the time the Captains were on shore they behaved with greatest politeness. The crews that came ashore with them were dressed in blue uniforms with cockades and made a genteel appearance, but all were armed with pistols. They had been out from Philadelphia ten weeks and had only taken four prizes."

In July the *Montgomery* captured a large English merchantman, the *Millern*, right on the Irish coast. There was rather sharp fighting for a glass and more. (A glass is the one-half hour required for one end of an hourglass to empty.) A prize crew was put aboard, and she was ordered to America, but on nearing the Delaware Capes was retaken by the British.

Shortly afterward, the *Montgomery* herself was captured by an English privateer, and outfitted as a privateer.

On August 6 the brig *Oliver Cromwell*, a Boston privateer under Captain Cole, captured two brigs. He wrote:

"One was formerly an American privateer called the *Montgomery* mounting 18 guns, taken and carried into Gibraltar. She had several Laidys on Board born to Lisbon whom we determined to take on Board us & c. together with our other Prisoners, land them (as they were effectionately desireous of it) on the British Shore. . . ."

Crews of captured English ships had to be taken care of. America had no such places as England's infamous Mill Prison at Plymouth, so they were kept at such places as could be provided. The treatment varied according to place and circumstances. Captain Henry Barnes and his crew were sent to Rhode Island when their ship was taken by the *Oliver Cromwell*. His letter of 1777 says, "We are treated with the greatest kindness and civility."

A prisoner wrote from Boston: "I bear it with patience. From the 3rd day of my captivity I have, with ninety others been confined a close prisoner in jail at this place lately erected called 'New Prison.' The Americans treat us very cavalierly—Unhappy War."

The frigate Randolph showing the Grand Union flag

The Continental Navy frigate *Randolph*, 32 guns, is a favorite with many who fancy the warships of the American Revolution. This could be for the reason that she was the only Continental Navy frigate to fly the Grand Union flag and the first to get to sea. The date of her launching was reported to be July 16, 1776. That it took a longer time to finish and fit her out than first estimated is evident from the fact that she was not ready to go to sea until late 1776.

Captain Nicholas Biddle was appointed to her command. Several times he had received orders to sail, but was prevented by the British blockade at the Delaware Capes and by ice in the river at Philadelphia where she was built.

But at last, on January 13, 1777, the Continental Navy vessels *Hornet, Fly,* and *Randolph* got safely past the British and out to sea, bound for the West Indies for supplies. Unfortunately, the *Randolph* had not proceeded farther than off Cape Hatteras when she was struck by a violent tempest in which two of her masts were sprung and ruined. She became separated from her consorts.

She had left Philadelphia greatly undermanned. Her crew should have numbered 350, but she had just somewhat more than half that complement. And of these, half had never been to sea before. Among those who had been were thirty English sailors who were prisoners of war and had been given their freedom in return for signing on. They were a troublesome lot and when their ship was in distress they started to mutiny. This could have been very serious but for the fact that the captain was the most experienced officer in the naval service. He at once employed the stern measures of the sea to quell the mutinous sailors.

Captain Nicholas Biddle was descended from an old family of West Jersey people. His father had moved to Philadelphia before Nicholas, his sixth son, was born in 1750. Young Biddle went to sea at age thirteen, was twice shipwrecked, went to England, and by means of letters from his family connections was rated a midshipman on board a Royal Navy sloop of war, commanded by Captain Sterling, who later became Admiral of the Fleet. An interesting fact about young Biddle is that he went on board one of the vessels under the Honorable Captain Phipps to the North Pole. Also on the cruise was a young volunteer like himself—Nelson, later Lord Nelson. Both served as coxswains by the commodore's appointment. This was in 1773 and difficulties with the American colonies were fast coming to a head. With war clouds threatening, Biddle returned to the land of his birth and offered his services to his country. His first command was a small sloop, then the *Andrea Doria,* which he took on the raid of New Providence Island as one of Commodore Hopkins' fleet. Back in America with his ship, he captained her on two very successful cruises in which valuable prizes were taken. As a reward, and because he was the only "trained" officer in the navy, he was given command of the *Randolph.*

The *Randolph* was about 155 feet long from tip to tip, beak to taffrail. Her bowsprit boom beyond would make a total of 195 feet end to end. The beam was 34 feet, and the draught of water 18½ feet. There was not much fancywork about her. It is not known if she had a figurehead. There was no other carving; she was the typical "workhorse" frigate of her day. This series of four paintings depicts the *Randolph* at different stages in her history.

The first Continental Navy frigate, the *Randolph*

The Continental Navy frigate *Randolph*, 32 guns, under Captain Nicholas Biddle, limped into Charleston, South Carolina, under jury sail. She was badly damaged from a gale that had hit her off Cape Hatteras on January 13, 1777. So she was not the "smart ship" that her young captain would have wanted to present to this fashionable seaport. Charleston was not a shipbuilding center, but was good at fitting out and repair work. For well over a hundred years, ships of the world had called at her docks. The *Randolph* was restored to seaworthiness, a crew was recruited, and orders were received from the Marine Committee to cruise in the West Indies and intercept a fleet of British merchantmen expected to sail from Jamaica about July 26.

The *Randolph* sailed sometime during the summer, and early in September was again off Charleston. Captain Biddle reported to his superiors:

"I have the pleasure to acquaint you that on the fourth of September 30 Leags. S.E. of Charles Town Barr I met with and took, after a little Resistance, the *True Britton*, Thomas Venture Master, of twenty six-pounders and seventy-four men; the Brig *Charming Peggy*, Capt. Lyon—both Laden with Rum for the British Army and Navy and bound from Jamaica to New York; the Ship *Severn*, Capt. Henderson, of eight, four-pounders, who had been taken by an American Cruizer on His passage from Jamaica to London And Retaken by the *True Britain*, Also a French Brig laden with salt going from the West Indies for Charles Town, Which Capt. Venture had made Prize of. There was a small Sloop in Company with those Vessels that made Her escape, the Weather being Squally, whilst I was Manning the Rest. I Arrived Safe here with my Prize the 7th inst. I have not laid Claim to Salvadge for the French Brig, as I thought it would be most agreeable to Congress to give her up. The *Randolph*'s Bottom is very foul, having lain in this Port the three worst Months in the Year since We Cleared: And Being apprehensive that the Worms will Ruin Her Bottom unless they are soon destroyed, I have thought Proper and am preparing to heave Her down. I shall be as expeditious as possible and hope to be Ready to execute any Orders You may Please to send by the Return of the Express. I cannot omit telling you that My Officers have on every Occasion given me the greatest Satisfaction. Two better Officers are not met in the Service than Barnes and McDougall, My first and second Leiuts. And the men I took from here behaved exceeding well."

In answer to his report, Captain Biddle received orders from the Marine Committee, dated October 24, 1777, to proceed to France as soon as his ship could be made ready for the voyage. Upon his arrival he was to report to the American commissioners at Paris for their instructions, and while waiting for these directions, to make a short cruise in European waters if it should seem advisable.

Charleston had a perfect place for careening ships—a mud flat in the Ashley River south of the city—and here the *Randolph* was hove down for the difficult job of scraping and redoing her bottom. Also, perhaps the social life of the city, which was not yet hurt by the war, was agreeable to Captain Biddle and the young officers.

The *Randolph* in the harbor at Charleston, South Carolina

Captain Nicholas Biddle of the Continental Navy frigate *Randolph* brought his ship and four prize vessels into the port of Charleston on October 1, 1777, to the delight and patriotic enthusiasm of the citizens of that fashionable city. The captain, a hero, and his officers were popular in the social circles, and Biddle became engaged to a Charleston belle.

After hoving his ship down for bottom work, Captain Biddle, following the orders of the Marine Committee, took his ship on a voyage to France, arriving at L'Orient in December. Her stay in French waters was not long; she returned to America, sailing directly for Charleston where the captain and ship could take their part in an action that had already been planned by the South Carolina Council of Safety and by Congress. This was to be a cruise to the West Indies for supplies and whatever trouble could be heaped on English ships encountered en route and returning to their base at Charleston.

Captain Biddle was to be in command of a squadron of vessels with the *Randolph* serving as flagship to the South Carolina State Navy cruisers: the ship *General Moultrie*, 18 guns; and the brigs *Notre Dame*, 16 guns; *Polly*, 16 guns; and *Fair American*, 14 guns. All vessels had full crews, and South Carolina furnished 150 troops to serve as marines.

After rounds of sendoff parties, balls, and celebrations, this task force squadron left Charleston. They were out of the river, past the bar, and at sea on February 12, 1778.

A number of British vessels had been reported cruising along the North and South Carolina coasts. This squadron hunted for them, but not finding them concluded that they had left. Then the fleet sailed for the West Indies, cruising several days to the east of Barbados. In Longitude 55° 20′, latitude 10° 30′, on the afternoon of March 7, the *Randolph* from her lookout sighted a large vessel to the windward, coming down with the wind. The *Randolph*, followed by her consorts, ranged up to see what sort of ship the stranger might be. By 8 P.M. she was up close and disclosed herself to be the British man-of-war H.B.M. *Yarmouth*. This 64-gun ship was twice the *Randolph* in guns and weight of metal, in crew, and in size.

When she was within gun range of the Americans she showed British colors and demanded to know who the *Randolph* was. The *Randolph* answered by running up the thirteen-stripe flag and by a resounding broadside of chain shot. The two ships were side by side, not much more than pistol range apart, and a fair wind behind them. A spirited exchange of fire began. Captain Biddle was wounded in the thigh at the first enemy fire, but continued to command from a chair on deck. The *Randolph*'s fire was rapid and accurate. According to a letter from the captain of the *Notre Dame*, the *Randolph* handled the *Yarmouth* so roughly for ten or twelve minutes that the Englishman must have shortly struck her colors, "Her sails being much cut up." At this moment of glory for the *Randolph*, a chance shot must have struck her powder magazine, for she exploded with tremendous force.

The engagement of the *Randolph* with the H.B.M. *Yarmouth*

The nighttime engagement between the Continental Navy frigate *Randolph,* 32 guns, under Captain Biddle, and H.B.M. *Yarmouth,* 74 guns, under Captain Vincent, occurred on March 7, 1778. It lasted for fifteen or twenty minutes, hot and furious, practically within pistol range. According to reports of witnesses the little American was cutting the big Britisher to pieces when the frigate blew up.

Perhaps all is best told in a letter from the captain of the *Yarmouth* reporting on March 17, 1778, to his admiral: "On the 7th instant at half past five P.M. discovered six sail in the S.W. quarter, on a wind standing to the northward; two of them ships, three brigs and a schooner. We were then 50 leagues due east of this island. We immediately bore down upon them and about nine got close to the weather quarter of the largest and headmost ship. They had no colors hoisted and as ours were then up, I hailed her hoist hers or I would fire into her, on which she hoisted American and immediately gave us her broadside, which we returned, and in about a quarter of an hour she blew up. It was fortunate for us that we were to windward of her; as it was, our ship was in a manner covered with parts of her. A great piece of a timber six feet long fell on our poop; another large piece of timber struck in our fore top gallant sail, then upon the cap. An American ensign, rolled up, blown in upon the forecastle, not so much as singed. Immediately on her blowing up, the other four dispersed different ways. We chased a little while two that stood to the southward and afterwards another that bore away right before the wind, but they were soon out of sight, our sails being torn all to pieces in a most surprising manner. We had five men killed and twelve wounded. But what I am now going to mention is something very remarkable. The 12th following, being then in chase of a ship steering west, we discovered a piece of wreck with five men on it waving; we hauled up to it, got a boat out, and brought them on board. They proved to be four men who had been in the ship which blew up and who had nothing to subsist on from that time but by sucking the rain water that fell on a piece of blanket which they luckily had picked up."

The rest of the colonial squadron arrived safely in port with a prize. The loss of the *Randolph* was a severe blow to the Continental Navy. The loss of her captain was an even greater setback to the American cause.

The *Andrea Doria* burning in the Delaware River

The brig *Andy Dora*—as the crew of the *Andrea Doria* called her—was one of the Continental Navy vessels that seemed always ready and able to carry out orders from the Marine Committee. With a vessel named *Surprise;* the sloop *Independence,* 10 guns; and the ship *Columbus,* 20 guns; the *Andrea Doria* was ordered in April, 1777, to clean Cape May Channel in New Jersey of British ships. In May she was reported blockaded in Narragansett Bay, but she was in the Delaware River when General Hower took possession of Philadelphia on September 26, 1777.

Admiral Howe, the general's brother, who had brought the British fleet around from the upper shore of the Chesapeake Bay after landing the army, arrived in Delaware Bay on October 4. The American forces still held the defenses of the river before Philadelphia—forts, naval vessels, and the famous obstruction in the river, the *cheval-de-frise*—sharp-ended logs ticking up at an angle below the waterline, held down with tons of rock. Fort Miffin was on Mud Island in the river, and Fort Mercer was on the New Jersey side. The Continental Navy vessels were the new frigate *Delaware,* 24 guns, the *Andrea Doria, Racehorse, Hornet, Wasp, Fly, Mosquito, Sachem, Repulse,* and *Champion,* and all of the Pennsylvania State Navy's vessels. They were under the command of Captain John Hazelwood.

The British, as soon as they were established in Philadelphia, erected two batteries on the city side of the river and to the southwest. The *Delaware* was anchored within a few hundred yards of one British battery. Unfortunately it became stuck on a mud flat and was lost to the British. They refloated and planned to take her into their navy. The H.B.M. *Roebuck* was in the van of the British men-of-war that came up the river. Fire from the forts backed up by actions of the naval vessels kept the enemy at bay for some days. By extreme effort they succeeded in making an opening in the *cheval-de-frise* despite fire from the guns of the American vessels. Their ships attempted to pass through the opening but were repulsed by the guns of the forts. The conflict continued November 1 when the enemy built up such heavy shore batteries that the Americans had nothing to match them.

The British had to have the river to make the vital supply line to their army in Philadelphia. There was a great attack on the American forces on November 10, but the worn Patriots held until a general assault on November 15. The Americans were driven from the Delaware River.

At this time David Bushnell, the inventor of the submarine, made his "keg torpedoes"—kegs filled with gunpowder with a contact firing device. They were not used successfully, however.

All American vessels up and down the river were destroyed. The Americans burned their two still-uncompleted frigates, the *Washington* and the *Effingham.*

Some small American craft succeeded in running past the British guns in Philadelphia, down the river, to the sea. The brig *Andrea Doria* was trapped anchored in midstream. Her crew took part of her sail; so many uses could be found for sailcloth. Then they set her afire and pulled away in their boats to look back. She burned to the water's edge and sank into the river.

The American privateer *Spy* fighting for a prize

The British Navy schooner H.M.S. *Prince William,* 8 guns, was captured and taken into the port of Boston. The captain of this vessel, wrote from prison on May 13, 1778: "In my last I acquainted you of my success in taking American prizes, but my fortune now is quite the reverse. On the 2d of this month, falling in with the *Spy,* an American privateer *Snow* of 12 guns, my vessel was taken after an engagement of three glasses and brought into this port, where myself and crew are prisoners. Boston harbor swarms with privateers and their prizes; this is a great place of rendezvous with them. The privateersmen come on shore here full of money and enjoy themselves much after the same manner the English seamen at Portsmouth and Plymouth did in the late war; and by the best information I can get there are no less than fifteen foreign vessels lately arrived in the harbor with cargos of various articles."

Here is the other side of the coin—a letter written by Captain Freeborn of the colonial privateer *Revenge,* which sailed from the island of Martha's Vineyard off Massachusetts for the West Indies December 9, 1777: "About ten days after, we fell in with a Privateer Schooner, gave her a couple of shot and she run. About 8 days after, we fell in with and took the ship *York* from Glasgow bound to Barbados, laden with dry Goods, some provisions, & c., which was sent into Martineer. About 4 days after, fell in with a large English Ship of 18 Guns, which was too much for us. We afterwards came across a fleet of about 100 Sail, to Windward of Barbadoes, but they being convoy'd by 5 Frigates and it blowing a hard gale, we could do nothing with them. We then bore away for Martineer, sprung our Mast and carried away our Topmast but luckily got in and found our Prize safe."

The term "privateer" as used to describe the activity of a vessel in the American Revolution meant an armed vessel not engaged in cargo carrying but devoted entirely to warlike use. "Letters of marque" were armed cargo carriers with papers from their government that made of them quasi-naval vessels. These terms were not too rigorously defined, and there was a degree of overlapping and confusion in their application.

Because a regulatory branch of the government issued the letters of marque, the number is known—about 1,500. The number of privateers is not known; it is estimated to have been 2,000 about during the years of the war. An example: Salem, Massachusetts, where a record was kept, sent out 158 private armed vessels. They were outfitted with about 2,000 guns, their crews numbered more than 6,000 men. They captured about 400 vessels and got nine of ten safely back to port.

The attraction of privateering was the money. A fat prize taken could mean a lifetime fortune to the vessel's owners and to the officers. Each member of the crew, down to the least, got his share. And, if taken by the enemy, the treatment of a privateersman was the same as that of a sailor of the regular navy.

There was usually an element of patriotism mixed with privateering, for the crews remembered that they represented a country fighting for her life, and they proudly showed the flag in the tradition of the sea. Warfare was changing. In 1776 the British still fought by the classical rules; the Americans were more effective at Indian-style warfare, and this was reflected at sea. In a typical action a privateer attempted to come up unobserved on the enemy, hail, raise the flag, and then fire.

The *Oliver Cromwell* putting a crew on board a prize

The hatred of King George III and his ministers for the rebelling Patriots led the Americans to express their feelings in the naming of their war vessels. They could think of no name expressing more spite toward the English Crown than that of the Lord Protector, Oliver Cromwell, and at least three American vessels of the Revolution days had this name.

One of them, a brig out of Beverly, Massachusetts, of which Captain William Cole was the master, carried 16 guns that in her voyages were heard in all ports of the Atlantic. With her crew of a hundred seafarers, she was out from 1777 until the war's end, and the great number of prizes taken made her a famous privateer.

The Connecticut State Navy's *Oliver Cromwell*, 20 guns, under Captain Timothy Parker, was one of the best of that state's five warships, and she flew the state flag to which was added thirteen stripes. Connecticut was the first to have a banner of her own. It was about the same as the present-day state flag, except for the colors. It had on a shield three flourishing grapevines representing Hartford, Windsor, and Wethersfield.

The exact dimensions of the *Oliver Cromwell* are not known, but she is thought to have been about 90 feet on deck, and to have a beam of from 25 to 27 feet. She was a most seaworthy ship. She cruised in company with the Connecticut Navy ship *Defence*, 18 guns. On April 15, 1778 they fell in with and captured the British ships *Admiral Keppel*, 18 guns, and *Cygnus*, 16 guns, near the Bahamas. How this engagement looked at firsthand is recorded in a letter by a seaman on the *Oliver Cromwell*:

"We engaged the ship *Admiral Keppel* as follows: When we came in about twenty rods of her, we gave her a bow gun. She soon returned us a stern chase then a broadside of grape and round shot. Captain orders not to fire until we can see the white of their eyes. We get close under their larboard quarter. They begin another broadside and then we began and held tuff and tuff for about two glasses, then she struck to us. At the same time the *Defence* engaged the *Cyrus*, who as the *Keppel* struck, wore round under our stern. We wore ship and gave her a stern chase, at which she immediately struck. The loss on our side was one killed and six wounded—one mortally —who soon died. Our ship was hulled nine times with six-pound shott, three of which went through our berth, one of which wounded the boatswains yeoman. Their larboard quarter was filled with shott—one nine pounder went through her main mast. Employed in the afternoon taking out the men and manning the prize."

Both ships sailed on cruises for the rest of the year, mostly in company. However, smallpox on board the *Defence* kept her at Charleston, South Carolina, for a month or more. In March, 1779, the *Defence* was wrecked on the coast of her state.

The *Oliver Cromwell*, on March 6, at nine in the morning, saw sail and gave chase; half an hour later the captain saw four other sails, three of them large ships. He then hauled close as they started in chase of his ship. He could tell that fighting would be inevitable and cleared his decks for action. The chase lasted until 4 P.M. when the *Oliver Cromwell* could no longer fight three enemies at the same time. "We hoped we had Done our Duty, we hoped we had done Enough to Convince our Enemies as well as Others that we Dare oppose them."

The Continental Navy sloop of war *Ranger*

Lieutenant John Paul Jones gave up the command of the Continental Navy's first flagship, *Alfred,* in December, 1776. He fully expected to be raised to the rank of captain, and to be given command of one of the new frigates under construction and soon to be in service. But he received neither, and he made his position and disappointment clear in an effective letter to Robert Morris of the Marine Committee.

It took a little time, but the Congress resolved two Acts on June 14, 1777. The first made the Stars and Stripes the official flag of the nation; the second gave Lieutenant John Paul Jones a captain's commission in the navy and command of the new sloop of war *Ranger,* 18 guns.

Jones went at once to Portsmouth, New Hampshire, to his new ship. She was 116 feet long on her gundeck; 34 feet beam; hold 13 feet 6 inches; 388 tons burthen; made for a crew of 150; built by James K. Hacket.

The *Ranger* was a fair, sturdy ship. Her name came from a volunteer military force raised in Massachusetts at the earliest part of the war. But this was an attractive name everywhere; there were four other ships called *Ranger* in the Revolution, one of which was British.

Captain Jones did not find his ship anywhere near ready, and the Marine Committee agent at Portsmouth was reluctant to turn her over to the new captain. He did so only inch by inch, making the takeover very disagreeable. An example concerns an important item, the sails. There were good sails to be had at Portsmouth at the time, but the agent would authorize only a "suit of Hessens," a material not much better than jute sackcloth.

Nevertheless Captain Jones waved farewell to land duty and sailed for France on November 1, 1777. He had not been to sea for eleven months. In making the Atlantic crossing the *Ranger* started her work. Two large enemy brigs were taken and sent to Nantes, where she herself was headed, arriving December 2. The ship had proved to be "crank" (wanting to go to the port side), and there were many defects in her design. Her masts and yards far too large and heavy; the rock ballast was troublesome.

Jones proceeded to cut down in size and restep the masts. He put in lead ballast and had new sails made of the finest French voile. New uniforms for the crew were brown; those for the officers were blue with white facings, not red. The *Ranger* was now a fighting ship.

While his ship was being reworked, Captain Jones made several visits to Dr. Benjamin Franklin in Paris, and the old gentleman must have recognized the qualities the young officer possessed. They became staunch friends. Captain Jones presented his ideas of taking the war to England, and Dr. Franklin approved and supported the plan. Dr. Franklin made him known to important people of France, which was of great benefit to the captain.

The *Ranger* left Nantes in February, 1778, going down the river and out into Quiberon Bay where there lay a great French fleet under Admiral La Motte-Picquet. Jones was determined to have his ship's flag recognized by a salute from the French, and after considerable prearranging, on February 14, with the sun shining and a fresh breeze, the French answered in salute to that fired in her honor by a small American sloop of war.

At that time this event was of utmost importance to the new nation across the water. Which of the several early United States flags the *Ranger* flew has never been settled; there is evidence both for the "Franklin Flag"—red, white, and blue stripes with no stars, and for the first formal flag adopted by Congress, which contained a circle of thirteen stars.

The *Ranger* engaged with the H.M.S. *Drake*

The Continental Navy sloop of war *Ranger* was in the best of fighting trim when she left the port of Brest, France, on April 10, 1778, but all was not right with the crew of 123 men. Unknown to Captain Jones, the senior lieutenant was in the employ of two of the American commissioners who were not on good terms with Dr. Franklin. This first officer on the *Ranger* was to promote mutiny among the crew, putting Captain Jones in a bad light and thereby reflecting on the good judgment of his friend, Dr. Franklin.

Thus, during the cruise Captain Jones had to contend with insubordination, which spoiled what should have been a successful venture right into the heart of the enemy's waters, the Irish Channel.

On April 14, off the Scilly Islands, a brig was taken and sunk. On the seventeenth, off Dublin, a ship was captured and sent to France. The *Ranger* then cruised for nearly a week near the Isle of Man where Captain Jones could see in the distance his early homeland of Scotland. Then, the ship crossed to the Irish side. From fishermen whose boat was captured it was learned that a British frigate, H.M.S. *Drake,* lay in the roads of Carrickfergus harbor.

Captain Jones devised a plan to run in and destroy this ship, but a sudden freshening wind caused the scheme to be abandoned. The *Ranger* crossed again to England. A daring raid on Whitehaven to burn the 200 and more coastal vessels in port was not a great success because part of the landing party did not follow orders. Also, an attempt to capture the Earl of Selkirk at his castle on St. Mary's Isle, off Cornwall, failed.

Captain Jones still had in mind a design on the enemy warship H.M.S. *Drake.* The *Ranger* again crossed the channel to the Irish side and stood in the harbor entrance in sight of the enemy ship. As expected, the *Drake* sent out a boat with an officer and four men, demanding to know who the stranger was. Captain Jones made this officer and men his prisoners and tied their boat to the *Ranger's* stern, knowing that the *Drake's* captain would come looking for them. It was not long after that the *Drake* could be seen lifting her anchor and starting out of the roads in the direction of the *Ranger,* working slowly against the tide, in a moderate breeze.

Captain Jones kept his ship end-on-end so that the enemy could see only her stern and could not know that she was a warship.

It was near sunset when the *Drake* got nigh to the leeward and a bit astern the *Ranger.* She hailed to demand the stranger's name. Captain Jones waited a few moments; then all of a sudden he put his helm down hard, ran up the flag and, as the *Ranger* turned a side to the enemy, answered with a broadside that shook the *Drake.* But the enemy was not slow to follow, and thus began a running ship-to-ship exchange of fire as hot and volcanic as the Irish Channel had ever seen or heard. It lasted one hour and four minutes, a fight between fairly equally matched warships.

Captain Jones could see that his guns were telling more and more on the enemy. Her sails were all shot up and split, rigging tangled and dangling, her yards—some of them—shot in two, hanging and swinging in the wind.

With her captain and first officer desperately wounded—they did not recover—and forty casualties among the crew, H.M.S. *Drake* struck her colors on May 24, 1778.

The *Ranger* spent the next day repairing wounds. Then, in company with the *Drake,* she returned around the north tip of Ireland to Brest. The senior lieutenant was under ship arrest.

The *Bon Homme Richard* fitting out at L'Orient, France

Captain John Paul Jones, commanding the *Ranger,* returned to Brest, France, bringing the prize won in battle, the British frigate *Drake.* Wherever in France the story of his victory had spread, he was the hero of the day. The *Ranger*'s first officer was under ship arrest, and his backers, two American commissioners, demanded his release. They made such a protest that Captain Jones resigned command of the ship.

From what is known of all this he was not too unhappy at giving up this command, since he had his sights set on the fine new frigate *Indien,* and this moment of success seemed the proper time to press his efforts to obtain that ship. He applied to Dr. Franklin for advice and aid. Together they started a concerted campaign to add her to the Continental fleet as had been originally planned.

The *Indien* was newly built at Amsterdam for the Continental Navy, but had been sold to the King of France, to the discomfiture of the Americans. She was one of the largest frigates in the world, carrying 40 guns.

Nine months were spent in the exchange of letters between Dr. Franklin and France about this ship. But he could not get her for his country. However, all was not lost. The French minister offered the best that his nation could spare to America, the fourteen-year-old *Duc de Duras,* veteran of the East India trade. She was unsound, a dull sailer at best, and not built or suited to be a warship.

Dr. Franklin advised his young friend Captain Jones to accept this ship and do with her the best he could. The captain followed the advice, taking the old ship on one condition—that she be named in honor of Dr. Franklin's world-famous book, *Poor Richard's Almanac,* known to the people of France as *Bon Homme Richard.* This name was chosen by John Paul Jones, and he was to make it one of the best known for generations of Americans to come.

The ship was purchased by the United States from her owners. France put up the money for the purchase and for the remodeling planned and supervised by Captain Jones. The work was carried out at the L'Orient navy yard.

Naval guns always required several months to make; therefore, this was the first item ordered. They were not delivered on time and the only guns that could be obtained were old, used barrels. A new main battery of 6 eighteen-pounders was fitted out in a new "gun room" on the lower deck of the ship's midsection. Two of these were the guns that burst at the first firing in the battle with H.B.M. *Serapis.* Gunports for them had to be cut in the ship's side, and they were too close to the waterline. In a rough sea, water got in.

It was intended that General Lafayette go on a cruise, to lead attacks on English posts. He would have 1,500 infantry, a body of cavalry, and several fieldpieces. To accommodate the general and his staff, Captain Jones had a large roundhouse built on the *Richard*'s stern. It was later determined that the general would not go, and it is believed that the roundhouse was then removed, since it took up too much deck space.

This ship must have looked like other East Indiamen of her time; she was the same size and type as those pictured in marine paintings and built into models of her day. It is known that Captain Jones was pleased with her high stern and quarters, which made the *Bon Homme Richard* look like a two-decker. Also, it is known that her hull was black, but the fancy carving of her stern, quarters, and head may have been in bright colors.

The *Bon Homme Richard* at start of battle with the H.B.M. *Serapis*

Five months were needed to remodel and outfit the *Bon Homme Richard* (40 guns) before she was ready to put to sea as the flagship of a squadron that was to cruise and raid the English coast. With her were three French war vessels, the *Pallas,* 32 guns; the *Cerf,* 18 guns; and the *Vengeance,* 12 guns; and the new Continental Navy frigate *Alliance,* 40 guns. This force left Groix on June 17, 1779. The second night out, in a senseless tack the *Alliance* fouled and broke the *Richard*'s bowsprit, and the ships had to return to port for the repair. This was the start of the endless trouble that Captain Pierre Landais, commander of the *Alliance,* was to make for the cruise. The fleet left the second time on August 14, going up west and across the north of Ireland, through the passages of the northern islands, then down the east coast of Scotland and England.

Over these miles the usual occurrences of a fleet at sea took place; ships separated and scattered, then rejoined. But the *Alliance* was always very far ahead or behind—an intentional violation of Captain Jones' orders. Many prizes were taken, some were sent to France, some were burned. The *Richard* had over 200 English prisoners in her orlop, the lower deck.

As the squadron moved down the Firth of Forth, Captain Jones started a raid on Leith, but in this he was not supported by the other captains and had to call off the undertaking.

From a captured pilot, Captain Jones learned that a great fleet of merchant sail was at that time moving along the coast, convoyed by two British war vessels, the H.B.M. *Serapis,* 44 guns, and the *Countess of Scarborough,* 22 guns. The American squadron, at Flamborough head, decided to wait there hoping to see the fleet. The next day, September 23, 1779, the fleet appeared bearing north-northeast.

On sighting the American squadron, the British warships put up flags to signal their fleet of sail to scatter for the coast. The American ships could see the two enemy naval vessels tacking to stand direct for them.

Captain Jones, knowing that there would be an engagement, took his station on the quarterdeck and gave orders to his men to clear the enemy's tops first, then sweep their decks with musket fire. To effect this, he put twenty men in the main top, fourteen in the fore, and ten in the mizzen top. The winds were light and the enemy had been some distance out when they started. It was after dark, 7:20 P.M., and the moon was up, before the foremost British ship, the *Serapis,* reached within hail of the *Richard* and demanded to know her name. "The *Royal Princess!*" was the answer. A moment passed. "Repeat the name or I will fire into you," came from the *Serapis.* The answer was several shot from the main top. The enemy returned with a thundering broadside. The *Richard* fired . . . there was a violent explosion, and a great hole opened in her gundeck. Two of the heavy guns below had burst, killing their crews, rendering at least three-quarters of her guns useless. Captain Jones realized that his ship was no match for the powerful adversary and he closed with her to board, but his men were beaten off. Now Jones turned his ship directly abeam the enemy's bow. The *Serapis* tried to avoid a collision but could not. She ran her bowsprit into the *Richard*'s starboard mizzenmast rigging.

Captain Jones sprang at the chance—he had the enemy's bowsprit lashed to his ship's mast. Each ship brought all guns available to bear on the other. They blazed away, and the fiercest battle of all the days of sail commenced.

The *Bon Homme Richard* and the *Serapis* in the heat of battle

The crew of the *Bon Homme Richard* was a mixed lot—fifty-seven Americans, thirty-seven French, thirty Portuguese, and eighty-three English, Irish, and Scotch, including Captain John Paul Jones. With others, the total came to 318. The crew of the *Serapis* was about the same in number, but only in this were the ships equal. The American ship was old, the English new. She was a late model, double-decked, rated at 44 guns carrying 52. Ship for ship she was far superior to the *Richard.* But in spite of her advantages, Captain Pearson, her commander, with her bowsprit jammed in the American ship's mizzenmast rigging, could not get her free.

Captain Pearson dropped anchor, thinking that might make the American drift away, but it did not—it only acted as a pivot. The bowsprit groaned, split and broke as wind and tide forced the two ships side by side. The Americans got two lines on the *Serapis,* and they were lashed, fouled, and bound together stem to stern as the guns thundered.

From the tops Captain Jones' men maintained such a hot musket fire that it drove all the enemy men below deck; only the captain and his officers kept to their stations. Below, however, the British had their own way. With the two ships touching, one against the other, they fired round after round of broadsides into the *Richard*'s middle decks, reducing her insides to splinters and pulp, many shots going all the way through the far side to fall into the water.

At some point in the din and roar the British captain thought he heard the Americans ask for quarter. "Do you strike?" he shouted into his trumpet. The answer came back from Captain Jones: "No, I have not yet begun to fight!"

Now the American frigate *Alliance* got into the battle, sailing around and around the engaged ships, firing broadsides not at the enemy but at the *Richard,* hitting her where it hurt most—between wind and wave. The reason for this has never been explained.

The main yardarms of one ship were over the deck of the other, and men from the Richard's top formed a human chain to pass bombs to a Frenchman on the end of the yard. He dropped the bombs onto the deck of the *Serapis* below, and he became so expert at this that he put one through the hatch to land below deck. It fell among some powder charges and set off such a damaging chain explosion as to stun those nearby who were not killed outright.

At the same instant as this explosion a gun crew on the *Richard*'s quarterdeck had trained the fire from their gun on the enemy's mainmast, each shot taking out a bite. The mast, top, yards, sails, and rigging crashed to the deck, and the *Serapis* was a crippled and battered ship.

It was now nearly ten o'clock at night; the battle had started at seven-thirty. The captain of the *Serapis* realized that Captain Jones was not disposed to do other than fight until both ships sank, and the English crew was shattered. With his own hands he lowered the British flag, for his men refused to expose themselves to fire from the American's tops.

Both ships had been on fire for some time; flames were spreading on the *Richard*, while on the *Serapis* the fire was soon put out. Water was pouring into the hull of the *Richard* from the shot holes in her hull and from seams that had opened up. Her sailing master, fearing for the lives of the over 200 prisoners confined on the *Richard*'s lowest deck, opened the hatch. Up swarmed the angry and frightened men, ready to take over the ship. Lieutenant Dale of the *Richard* and a few others of the crew held the prisoners at gunpoint, ordering them to "Man the pumps or sink—fight the fire or burn."

Last moments of the sinking of the *Bon Homme Richard*

The fiercest battle of all known history between two sailing ships had come to a slow end, and it took several minutes to get word passed to the crews of both ships, the *Bon Homme Richard* and the *Serapis,* that the British ship had surrendered. As soon as some order was restored, Captain Jones received Captain Pearson on the shattered decks of the *Richard* for the formal surrender. A prize crew from the American ship under Lieutenant Dale was placed on and took command of the captured British ship. The lashings that had bound the ships together during the battle were cut so that the *Serapis* could move away from the danger of the burning *Richard.*

All attention was given to fighting the fire which the guns of the *Serapis* had started by shooting pointblank into the *Richard*'s side. Some shots had come from a distance of two feet. No one could get near the flames to extinguish them during the fighting, and they had spread. As a safety measure all powder in the magazine was removed to the quarterdeck. The *Richard* was also taking in water at an alarming rate. Seams that had opened during the pounding which the ship had taken from the British guns, and the shot holes from the guns of the frigate *Alliance* were letting in water faster than her pumps could work it out. A long night of fire fighting lay ahead of the crew that had fought the enemy since 7:30 P.M., and a long night of pumping lay ahead of the men who had been prisoners on the *Richard*'s lowest deck during the battle.

Lieutenant Dale and his crew on the *Serapis* had been clearing the decks—a tremendous scene of carnage, wreck, and ruin. The fallen mast and sail and the tangled rigging made their task equal to that performed on the *Richard.*

During the battle, at not too great a distance, Captain Cottineau of the *Pallas* had fought, defeated, and captured the British sloop *Countess of Scarborough,* and now he brought his ship and the prize to aid Captain Jones.

That the British Navy would be out in force looking for him was another worry of the American commander. With the lights on England's coast still in sight, many on shore had seen the glare of the battle. They would try to get word to the navy. It was of the greatest importance to get some type of jury sail up on the *Serapis* so she could get under way, and daylight was welcome. It was to be a hazy, muggy day with only light airs to fill the jury sails of the *Serapis.* Only her foremast was still intact, and she moved very slowly. The *Richard* still had all her masts, but she was low in the water. So as not to get too far ahead, the *Pallas, Countess,* and *Cerf* were under reefed sail; even the *Alliance* now joined the squadron again. The fire on the *Richard* was under control, but all that day and all that night her pumps worked. The next day, September 25, was again one of hazy, indifferent weather.

Captain Jones had admitted to no one but himself that there was no hope for the *Richard* until the carpenter reported that water was gaining on them. Then the captain ordered all living things aboard, including the coop of chickens, to be put aboard the *Serapis,* now flying the Continental flag. Eastward toward Holland the squadron crawled through the sea, holding back to stay near the noble *Bon Homme Richard.* Bow first she gently settled below the lapping waves. At twelve o'clock high noon her masts dipped below the water and she sank into the North Sea and into history.

The Continental Navy *Alliance* escapes the enemy

The *Alliance*, 36 guns, and her sister ship the *Confederacy* were the largest frigates of the Continental Navy. Exact measurements and details of the *Alliance* are not known; therefore, those of her sister ship are employed to reconstruct her appearance. What records there are of her indicate that she was not as beautifully finished and fitted out as her sister, but she had one feature possessed by only a very limited number of ships—she was a "halcyon," a lucky and happy ship.

Built in 1777 by James and William Hacket on the Merrimack River at Salisbury, Massachusetts, the *Alliance* became the "favorite of the people," as popular as *"Old Ironsides"* was to be years later. She was the only frigate to go all the way through the war and be afloat when the peace treaty was signed. She was "sold out" of the navy in 1785 and was made into a packet, remaining in service for several years. She sank in the Delaware at Philadelphia about 1800.

When the *Alliance* first received sailing orders, her commander was Pierre Landais, a former French Navy officer who had been given a captain's commission by the Continental Congress on the recommendation of Silas Deane. His instructions were to proceed to France, where he was ordered to join the squadron commanded by Captain John Paul Jones on the cruise around the British Isles that began June 17, 1779.

Captain Landais' strange behavior in having his ship's guns fire broadsides at the *Bon Homme Richard* while she was in combat with H.B.M. *Serapis* was unexplainable. When Captain Jones got the ships of his squadron and his prizes safely in Holland, he dismissed Captain Landais from duty and took command of his ship.

The other vessels of the squadron and the prizes had gone on to France, but in the winter of 1779, the *Alliance* was still anchored in the Texel in northern Holland. Captain Jones had used the time since he took her command to put her in fighting trim, and she was ready for the sea. Five British Navy war vessels, including two frigates, cruised the waters of the Texel, keeping an eye on the *Alliance*. The British ambassador so strongly protested to the government of Holland for allowing this American rebel ship in their harbor that the Dutch authorities had no other choice but to order Captain Jones to leave at once. That meant he would be forced to sail his ship right into the face of the British guns, a prospect that was in no way appealing. He stalled and begged, saying that he would leave as soon as all the water could be pumped from the ship's hull and the leak fixed. He gave any excuse at all.

The winter weather was about to turn thick and nasty. A gale from the northeast was moving in and ships in the harbor were hove to and battened down to face the blow. The English warships were all boxed in to ride out the storm.

In the early morning of December 27 the wind had started to howl and the sea to roll and toss. With all at the ready, guns rolled out and men at their stations, Captain Jones slipped his ship's cables. Out she dashed, past the amazed harbor master's craft, past the waiting British frigates, down the North Sea into the English Channel, past the Downs—the great British fleet was at Spithead—past Plymouth into the Atlantic. The *Alliance* did not stop until she was in the safe harbor of Groix. Captain Jones had saved her, and only once again was she ever to be in such a tight spot. Then, fortunately, there was another real master mariner on her deck, Captain John Barry.

The frigate *Ariel* in a tempest off the coast of France

Dr. Benjamin Franklin, more than forty years older than Captain John Paul Jones, possessed the great gift of being able to mollify flaring tempers, and it is likely that he had to utilize this talent when advising the naval hero. After the victory of the *Bon Homme Richard* over the H.B.M. *Serapis,* Captain Jones dismissed the commander of the Continental frigate *Alliance,* Captain Landais. He took command of that vessel himself, snatching it out of the very teeth of the British Navy to bring it safely to France. Captain Landais was waiting there to make whatever trouble he could for Captain Jones. In this he had the support of the American commissioners Arthur Lee and John Adams. They missed no opportunity in attempting to discredit Dr. Franklin, and acting against Captain Jones was one link in their chain of malicious schemes. They succeeded in having Captain Landais restored to the command of the *Alliance.* This left Captain Jones without a ship.

He still wanted the frigate *Indien* and with Dr. Franklin's aid attempted to get it for his command. This could not be done because the South Carolina Navy had already leased it for their service.

The French Navy, at Dr. Franklin's behest, offered the United States Navy a very good ship, the English frigate *Ariel,* 24 guns, which had been captured only a few months before on the coast of North Carolina. Captain Jones was advised by his mentor to take it, and he did. When the *Ariel* was fitted out to the captain's satisfaction, he was ordered to proceed to America with a cargo of military supplies for General Washington's army.

Just at this time Captain Jones' life was brightened by the King of France bestowing on him the Cross of Military Merit and presenting him with one of the most exquisite swords ever made. To receive these great honors he had to obtain the permission of the Continental Congress, and again Dr. Franklin paved the way.

The *Ariel* was heavily laden with her valuable cargo of arms and gunpowder, so Captain Jones delayed departing from port until after the fall storms had passed, hoping to have favorable weather for the passage. There was a promise of fair weather and smooth seas when the ship left Groix on October 8, 1780. But by the following night she was in the most violent tempest to hit the Atlantic coast of Europe in the memory of man. Before the masts could be cut away, the wind and water took them, and with them rails, the wheel, the boats, and part of the quarter deck. Each mountain of water drove the *Ariel* ever closer to the Penmarch Rocks, as dangerous a ledge as there is in any sea. The water she was in was not deep enough to run before the wind, and each wave that stood her on her beam ends could have marked her last moment. For three nights and two days the unrelenting storm kept the crew constantly at work to obey the watchful captain's stern orders.

The *Ariel* rode out this storm, but when it abated, she had neither masts nor rudder. Nevertheless she was not leaking—she was afloat, her cargo intact.

The captain knew that without a rudder she would go best stern first, so under jury sail she backed all the way to the port of L'Orient, France.

For miles around, the coast was strewn with the wreckage of ships; few lived through that storm. To seafaring men it was known that John Paul Jones was the very master in the ways of a ship.

The *Ariel* was repaired; she landed General Washington's arms and gunpowder in Philadelphia on February 18, 1781.

Fitting out the Continental Navy ship *America*

The enthusiasm for naval construction legislation reached its highest peak on November 2, 1776, when the Continental Congress resolved to build a number of vessels, among these to be three 74-gun ships. One was built—the *America*—at Rising Castle Island in the river before Portsmouth, New Hampshire. Her upper deck length was more than 180 feet; her beam was 50 feet; her draught was about 25 feet. She measured from the end of her boom to the back of her taffrail more than 300 feet. Her keel was laid down in May, 1777. Five years later she was launched, on November 5, 1782. This length of time indicates that there were many difficulties attending her building. The major problems were shortage of money and materials and loss of interest.

The Marine Committee realized that having only one such ship was to no purpose—a fleet of twenty or more might have been useful, but the young nation simply could not challenge Great Britain on the sea with one 74-gun ship. So work went along ever so slowly, and she was almost forgotten by the Congress.

After an absence of three years Captain John Paul Jones returned to America on the ship *Ariel*, laden with arms and gunpowder, arriving at Philadelphia in February, 1781. The *Ariel* was to be returned to France, and the Congress had no ship for him to command. He had heard that a 74-gun ship was being built, and evidently he asked to be made captain of her, for Congress, by a unanimous vote, made him the ship's commander.

This was in August, and he went at once to Portsmouth to supervise her completion. He had been led to believe that the ship was ready for launching, but to his surprise and astonishment, he found that the hull was only partly built. When he recovered from the disappointment, he pitched in with his customary zeal to prepare the ship for sea. There was no end of his enthusiasm at the very thought that this would be the world's largest 74-gun warship.

Further delays could not be prevented. Lack of money and shortage of materials, plus the inexperience of those employed to work on her, forced him to institute a training course for most of the workmen.

Several times the British had sent boats of landing parties up the Piscataqua River with the intention of burning the ship on the stocks. Armed citizens had driven them off. Now that work was progressing, Captain Jones thought that a full-time armed guard of some force was needed with alarm lookouts stationed along the river to report an invasion. This was put into effect and the guard was once alerted to repel a landing party with gunfire.

Captain Jones had been in Portsmouth for a year. To his other credits must be added that he had the ship, which was now named *America*, ready for launching.

In their aid to the American cause of freedom and liberty, the French had lost the *Magnifique*, a 90-gun ship of the line, aground in Boston harbor. After the victory at Yorktown, the attitude of the Congress toward the great French nation changed for the better and as a gesture of appreciation they voted to give to France the new ship *America* to replace the one lost: "Resolved that the agent of marine be and he is hereby instructed to present the *America*, a 74-gun ship in the name of the United States, to the Chevalier de la Luzerne for the service of His Most Christian Majesty."

Captain John Paul Jones' last war service to his new country was to launch the *America* and turn it over to the French representative. The ship was completed and fitted out by the French at Portsmouth and went to sea. But her life was short; for owing to all the years her timbers had stood on the stocks, they were unsound. She was broken up in 1786.

The frigate *Hancock* firing a morning gun

The Continental Navy's *Hancock*, 32 guns, was as fine a frigate as was built anywhere in the last quarter of the eighteenth century, and the fastest sailer in the world. She must have been a beautiful ship. All parts were in perfect balance, and she had just the right amount of carving to set her off. Her graceful quarters and stern were an example of the Georgian flowing line, which greatly pleased the eye. As agreeable as this may have been to see, she was a fighting ship with a record equaled by only a few others. But this record was made not by the Americans who built her but by the British Navy which captured her and commissioned her into the Royal Navy under the name of H.M.S. *Iris.*

The *Hancock* and her little sister the *Boston* were built at the same time, at the same yard, the work of one shipbuilder. They were fitted out and went to sea together. For the time that the *Hancock* served the American cause they cruised in company. But unfortunately the fine work of so many hands that had united to create these vessels was placed with men who were serving the same cause but who were in total disagreement.

Captain Manley was appointed to command the *Hancock;* Captain McNeill the *Boston.* Their lack of accord was obvious to many, for example, to Dr. Samuel Cooper. His forebodings were recorded in a letter written to John Adams on April 3, 1777: "Manley and McNeill do not agree. It is not, I believe, the fault of the first. If they are not better united, infinite damage may acrue." Another letter to Adams, this time from Dr. William Gordon: "The frigates have been sailed a fortnight. Maritime affairs have been most horridly managed. We have beaten G. B. in dilatoriness and blunders. Where the fault hath

lain I know not but the credit of the Continental and the Congress requires amendment."

These ships sailed from Boston May 21, 1777, in the company of a fleet of privateers which by choice parted from the frigates the next day. The captains did not agree on anything, and the cruise is a day-by-day account of negative and nullifying minor events. They did however jointly capture a British frigate, the H.M.S. *Fox,* 28 guns. In the battle this vessel and the *Hancock* were pretty well shot up, but it was the *Boston* that did the fighting and firing. On July 16 the American ships with their prize the *Fox* fell in with the British men-of-war H.B.M. *Rainbow,* 44 guns and *Flora,* 32 guns. Only the *Boston* escaped. Her captain was charged with not giving any support of consequence, but he maintained that the *Hancock* had struck her colors at the sight of the British warships, and therefore he had no chance to assist her.

The *Hancock* was 161 feet from her head to the stern rail, and 35 feet in the beam. At the stern she was about 21 feet above the water, 10 feet at the waste, and 15 feet at the head. She drew 17 feet of water. Her builder was an old established firm at Newburyport, Massachusetts—Greenleaf and Cross. The plans for her construction did not arrive in time for them to be used when the ship was laid down. As a result, she was more the builders' product than the Marine Committee's design. In the Royal Navy, as the *Iris,* she chased and captured the American frigate *Trumbull* in 1781, then she herself was captured by the French in the West Indies. The English recaptured her in the Napoleonic Wars, but by then she was just an old hulk. Nevertheless, she was the last remnant of the Continental Navy to remain afloat.

The Continental Navy frigates *Hancock* and *Boston*

The Continental Navy frigates *Hancock,* 32 guns, and *Boston,* 24 guns, were assigned by the Congressional Resolution of December 13, 1775 to be built in Massachusetts Bay. Samuel Adams wrote to John Adams:

"I know it gives you great pleasure to be informed that this Congress have ordered the Building of thirteen ships of War, viz. five of 32 guns, five of 28, three of 24. I own I wished for double or treble the Number, but I am taught the Rule of Prudence, to let the fruit hang till it is ripe, otherwise those Fermentations in the political which like Error is said to produce in the natural Body. . . .

"Our Colony is to build two of these ships. We may want Duck [canvas]—I have been told that this article is manufactured in the counties of Hampshire & Berkshire—you may think it worth your enquiry—Our fleet which has been preparing here will be ready to put to Sea in two or three days and it is left to the Board of Admirallty to order its Destination—May Heaven succeed the Undertaking—Hopkins is appointed Commander in Chiefe—I dare promise that he will on all Occasions distinguish his Bravery, as he always has, and do honor to the American Flag."

This letter indicates the importance and dependence that were placed on the navy. Both Samuel and John Adams spent a great deal of time and energy on the legislative affairs of the Continental Navy when the program was first started.

Also greatly concerned were the British. Their intelligence agent made this report to Admiral Howe, describing the frigate *Hancock:*

"A Man's Head with Yellow Breeches, white stockings, Blue Coat with Yellow Button Holes, small cocked Hat with a Yellow Lace, has a Mast in lieu of an Ensign Staff with a Latteen Sail on it, has a Fore and Aft Driver Boom, with another across, Two top Gallant Royal Masts, Pole mizzen topmast, a whole Mizzen Yard and mounts 32 Guns, has a Rattle Snake carved on the Stern, Netting all around the Ship, Stern Black and Yellow, Quarter Galleries all Yellow. Principal Dimensions of the Rebel Frigate Hancock. Length on upper deck, 140 ft 8 ins. Breadth on Do. 30.2 length of Keel for Tonnage, 116.2 3/4. Extreme Breadth, 35.2. Depth in the Hole 10.7 Burthen in Tons, 764. Height between Decks, 5.6 Do in the Waste, 5.0. Size of the Gun Ports, fore & aft, 2.7. up & down 2.2. Length of the Quarter Deck, 57.8. Length on the Forecastle, 31.3. Draught of Water, afore 14.0. abaft 15.10."

Then for the frigate *Boston:* "An Indian Head with a Bow and Arrow in the Hand, painted White, Red and Yellow, Two top gallant Royal Masts, Pole mizzen topmast on which she hoists a Top gallant Sail. . . ."

Such complete information must have come from an inside informer, a Tory and a Loyalist—the other side of the coin from Patriot Samuel Adams.

The frigate *Boston* in a gale

The Continental Navy frigates *Boston, Warren, Providence, Deane,* and *Queen of France,* two Massachusetts State Navy cruisers, and ten large letters of marque were in Boston harbor in the middle of December, 1777. All were inactive because they had no crews. Privateering had made it practically impossible to get men. Nearby at Salisbury the new frigate *Alliance* was being fitted out, to face the same problem.

The *Boston* had a new commander, Captain Samuel Tucker. He did get together a shorthanded crew. The ship's journal for the date February 13, 1778, relates: "Capt. Tucker went to Braintree in his barge and brought the Hon. John Adams and suite on board." This distinguished passenger had been appointed commissioner to France to replace Silas Deane. With him was his son, John Quincy Adams, age eleven. They sailed February 15, with wind from the west southwest; on the 20th it was blowing a gale. "A clap of thunder with sharp lightning broke upon the main mast just above the upper moulding, which burnt several of the men on deck. A most terrible night. The main mast foreman was killed by lightning."

A British 36-gun frigate that had been in chase had been left behind by the swift *Boston.* Captain Tucker had instructions not to risk the ship in any way that might endanger Mr. Adams and was ordered to land him safe in France or Spain. Captain Tucker was a very experienced mariner; he knew how to give or obey orders, but when his ship fell in with the English brig *Martha* on March 10 at 11 P.M., the American colors were run up and the guns rolled out. Shots were fired and the brig struck; however, one of her shots had carried away the *Boston*'s mizzen yard. Boats from the *Boston* were got out at once with prize crews, but the rough seas prevented the

men from reaching the enemy ship before its crew had thrown the mail overboard. The *Martha* carried 16 guns, she was from London, bound for New York. The prize master took her to Boston where her cargo was valued at £97,000.

Rough weather accompanied the *Boston* all the way to Europe. She was never under full sail, but she arrived safe in the Garonne River in France on March 31. Here she was careened and had refitting work done. Her crew was filled out with Frenchmen when she went in company with some French vessels on a cruise in the Bay of Biscay. The mixed crew caused Captain Tucker trouble, and he was rid of it by August 1, when the *Boston* sailed for and anchored at Saint-Nazaire. With the *Boston* in France were the Continental Navy frigates *Ranger* and *Providence.* All sailed for America on September 26, and arrived on October 13 at Portsmouth, having taken three prizes on the crossing.

The *Boston* was a most dependable warship when under a good master. Her days were filled with cruising where and when ordered. With the *Deane* she took eight prizes in July, 1779, and got back to Boston harbor with 200 prisoners including a lieutenant colonel, a major, and three Royal Navy captains.

On September 21 she received instructions to be fitted out and provisioned at once and to proceed southward to Bermuda under sealed orders. When the orders were opened, they directed the ship to Charleston, South Carolina, to be part of Commodore Whipple's squadron in the unsuccessful defense of that important naval station. She was captured by the British and taken into their navy with her name changed to H.M.S. *Charlestown.*

The Continental Navy frigate *Raleigh* going close to the wind

The naval records of the frigate *Raleigh,* 32 guns, would tell that she was 131 feet 5 inches on berth deck, and 34 feet 5 inches in the beam, but the overall space that she would have taken up at a dock would exceed 200 feet in length. She was built near Portsmouth, New Hampshire, by James K. Hacket, James Hill, and the shipwright Stephen Paul. They worked under the very watchful eye of John Langdon, a local politician who had been, or was, a delegate to the Continental Congress; his business was shipowner. From his letters there is a sense that he was very conscientious, undertaking his work with utmost attention and seriousness. One of the first things he did was organize one hundred of the carpenters at the shipyard into an armed guard—to be ready to stand off the British by force if they attempted a raid.

Plans of the ship from the Marine Committee had not arrived by February 29, 1776, and Mr. Langdon did not want to wait any longer to get started, so he informed the committee that he would use his own plans. The result was one of the best frigates built—a favorite with marine enthusiasts until this day. Anyone wanting to know how long it took to build such a ship can refer to the New Hampshire *Gazette* for May 25, 1776:

"On Tuesday the 21st inst. the Continental frigate of thirty-two guns, built at this place under the direction of John Langdon, Esq., was Launched amidst the acclamation of many thousand spectators. She is esteemed by all those who are judges that have seen her—to be one of the compleatest ships ever built in America. The unwearied diligence and care of three Master-Builders—Messrs: Hacket, Hill and Paul, together with Mr. Thompson under whose inspection she was built, and the good order and industry of the Carpenters deserve particular notice; scarcely a single instance of a person being in liquor, or any difference among men in the yard during the time of her building—every man with pleasure exerting himself to the utmost; and altho' the greatest care was taken that only the best of timber was used and the work perform'd in a most masterly manner, the whole time from her raising to the day she launched did not exceed *sixty working days,* and what offered a most pleasing view (which was manifest in the countenance of spectators) this noble fabrick was compleatly to her anchors in the main channel in less than six minutes from the time of the run, without the least hurt; and what is truly remarkable, not a single person met with the least accident in launching, tho' near five hundred men were employed in and about her when run off."

Two months had been required to build and launch the hull, another month or less would have seen her fitted out. Now came a difficult task for all of the Continental shipbuilders—acquiring cordage, guns, and sailcloth, and Mr. Langdon was begging this person, then that, for sailcloth. In a letter to Nicholas Brown: "I am informed you have Some Canvas which can Spare, for the Ship I am buildg for the United Colonies at Portsmouth New Hampshire, shall take it kind if you'll be good enough to forward immediately in waggons one hundred and fifty Bolts of all Sorts, or of Such as you have, as the Sendg it by land is the only way you'll please order. The Carts to bring it from your place thru' Cambridge. . . ."

He didn't get the sailcloth; it took until the next year, July, 1777, before the *Raleigh* had her rigging sails.

The *Raleigh* attacking the H.M.S. *Druid*

Building the frigate *Raleigh* started out well, from the time her keel was laid down, on March 21, 1776, until she was launched exactly two months later. Then work went slower and slower, and it was mid-August before she got to sea, Captain Thomas Thompson her commander.

The British Navy was so large and formidable and the American Navy so small a force that the Marine Committee in charge did not know what to do with their ships. They could always send them for supplies, to the West Indies or to France. It was to these places that the *Raleigh* and the *Alfred* were ordered. They had a good run off the American coast and three small prizes were taken. On September 2 they captured the British snow *Nancy* which had, owing to some mishap aboard, dropped out of a large fleet of sail bound for the West Indies. Captain Thompson learned this from his prisoners, and from other information that they gave, determined the position of the fleet and that it was convoyed by the warships *Camel, Druid, Weasel* and *Grasshopper*.

The American ships crowded on sail and started in pursuit of the fleet, hoping to pick out a few strays. The next day the *Raleigh* sighted the fleet from her masthead, and both she and the *Alfred* put up all the sail they had so as to catch up with them.

Captain Thompson had learned their signals from the sailing master of the captured *Nancy*. Through the night the Americans trailed this fleet as best they could, for the wind had shifted, now putting them to the leeward of the fleet. At daylight the wind freshened and the *Alfred* had to shorten sail, thereby dropping be-hind, so Captain Thompson decided that any attempts on the fleet would have to be made by the *Raleigh* alone.

It was a dark day and the American stood boldly in among the British, getting on the weather side of a large merchantman, giving her a signal to move to the leeward so that she—the *Raleigh*—could come up on the warship directly ahead. The *Raleigh* in her short time at sea had proved herself a fine sailer, and almost without effort Captain Thompson had ranged up to a sloop of war, showing the fleet signal so that she would be taken as one of the fleet's own number. She ranged right alongside the English man-of-war.

The sea was rough and pitching, but at a favorable moment the *Raleigh* ran up her colors and opened with a broadside on the surprised enemy. The enemy were thrown off guard so completely that all aboard were in total confusion. The American followed with a telling rapid fire. The English ship started to return rather feeble fire and was getting herself in some order when a violent squall struck, parting the *Raleigh* from her opponent and for a few moments blotting out everything.

When the worst part of the squall had passed, the convoy could be seen steering in all directions, and the other warships of the convoy were bearing down on the *Raleigh*. Captain Thompson ran to the leeward, outdistancing them, until they gave up the chase to rejoin their fleet. He found the *Alfred* and in company they resumed their voyage to France.

The English sloop of war was the H.M.S. *Druid,* 24 guns. She had to limp back to England.

The *Raleigh* and *Alfred* in the roads of Brest, France

In the short fight with the *Druid*, Captain Thompson of the Continental Navy frigate *Raleigh*, 32 guns, had found a good spirit among his men. They were a shorthanded crew—not much more than half the number needed to make a full complement. The *Alfred* was the same, and since she lacked the sailing qualities of the new frigate, Captain Thompson determined to stay close to her and not seek unknown hazards of war.

At length they arrived in France. Both ships were in need of attention to their hulls and required refitting work. France had great shipyards on her Atlantic coast, and nearly all of the American vessels that voyaged to France took advantage of these facilities, especially to have new suits of sail made from the fine French cloth. They also acquired new cordage, the best, from Italy, and guns: the *Raleigh* needed 6 to fill out her 32.

Work on the ships and getting the supplies together to bring back to America took until February 28, 1778, when the *Raleigh* and *Alfred* again sailed in company for home by way of the African coast and the West Indies. They captured a British merchantman off Senegal.

By March 9 they had reached latitude 16° 31′ N, longitude 55° 40′ W. At 6 A.M. two sails were seen to the northwest. At half past seven the *Raleigh* hove to for the *Alfred* to catch up. The strangers were standing to the north, close hauled. The American vessels then hauled on the wind on the same tack with the other ships, which were to the leeward. Captain Thompson thought that this maneuver would give him more time to discover their force and sailing rate; he had already determined that they were armed.

The unknown ships then tacked as though to get through the wakes of the Americans. The *Alfred* was falling to the stern and to the leeward, and as the weathermost ship passed under her lee, her captain hoisted his colors and fired several guns. The fire was returned under English colors. At this time the *Raleigh* was almost three miles from the *Alfred* and could see her engaging the British ship, then setting all sail to escape. The two enemy ships could then be seen closing on the *Alfred*. Considering where he was, Captain Thompson concluded that he could not reach the *Alfred* before she would be forced to strike her colors. Therefore he dropped his courses, leaving the *Alfred* to her fate—surrender. The British men-of-war were the *Ariadne*, 20 guns, and *Ceres*, 16 guns.

The *Raleigh* arrived safe in America; Captain Thompson answered as well as he could at his court-martial for not supporting the *Alfred*. His only defense was that his ship was at a great distance from the *Alfred*. It was pointed out that this ship, with 20 guns, and his with 32 were more than a match for the enemy guns. That the *Alfred*'s sailing qualities were in question was offset by the fact that under Lieutenant John Paul Jones, this flagship of the first navy of the United States accounted for herself very well in outrunning several British vessels.

Captain Thompson was a good seaman and had spent all his life as a mariner. He had been the supervisor of the *Raleigh* when that ship was on the stocks. He had been raised to take care of his ship rather than risk her loss.

The *Alfred* was not soon forgotten. Many, for years to come, remembered the time when she was an object of pride and hope for the nation. Records are not clear as to what happened to her in British hands.

The Continental Navy frigate *Raleigh* at Boston harbor

Captain John Barry was appointed to command the frigate *Raleigh* on May 30, 1778, and sailed from Boston September 25. Wind was fresh at the northwest and the ship's first course was east by south. Two sails, at a distance, were sighted at noon. The *Raleigh* hauled to the north and the strangers did the same. They were the British warships H.B.M. *Experiment,* 50 guns and H.M.S. *Unicorn,* 22 guns. When a haze cleared the next day, they were seen in chase, and thus began a pursuit off the coast of Maine that lasted nearly seventy-five hours. The fast *Raleigh* at times sailed at a speed of over eleven knots. Three times she cleared her decks for action before a shot was fired. In changing tack several times some low rocky islands were seen to the west, not identified by the captain at the time. When the action started, it was as told by one of the *Raleigh*'s junior officers:

". . . the enemy hoisted the St. George's ensign. She appeared to be pierced for twenty-eight guns, we gave her a broadside, which she returned; the enemy then tacked and came up under our lee quarter and the second broadside she gave us, to our unspeakable grief, carried away our fore top mast and mizzen top gallant mast. He renewed the action with fresh vigor and we, notwithstanding our misfortune, having in a great measure lost command of our ship, were determined for victory. He then shot ahead of us and bore away to leeward. By this time we had our ship cleared of the wreck. The enemy plied his broadsides briskly, which we returned as brisk; we perceiving that his intentions were to thwart us, we bore away to prevent his raking us, and if possible to lay him aboard, which he doubtless perceived and having the full command of his ship prevented us by sheering off and dropping astern, keeping his station on our weather quarter. Night coming on we perceived the stern-most ship [*Experiment*] gaining on us very fast, and being much disabled in our sails, masts and rigging and having no possible view of escaping, Captain Barry thought it most prudent with the advice of his officers, to wear ship and stand for the shore, if possible to prevent the ship's falling into the enemy's hands by running her on the shore. The engagement continuing very warm about twelve mid-night saw the land bearing N.N.E. two points under our bow. The enemy, after an engagement of seven hours, thought proper to sheer off and wait for his consort, they showing and answering false fires to each other."

The *Unicorn* and *Experiment* joined in firing on the *Raleigh,* first one, then the other, then both at the same time. The Americans fired back with all the guns they could bring to bear on the enemy but their ship was now getting too close to the rocky shore for them, and they sheered off. Captain Barry ran the *Raleigh* onto the rocks. The enemy moved up to renew their fire; the *Raleigh* answered with her four stern pieces and soon after the enemy ceased fire until daylight.

Captain Barry, on finding that the shore lent itself to defense, decided to put his men and guns on shore, burn the ship, and fight it out on the land. Landing crews were engaged, and Captain Barry left the ship to direct the work. In his absence a petty officer of the *Raleigh,* an Englishman, signaled to the enemy that the Americans would surrender. They took the *Raleigh* but Captain Barry and many of his men onshore escaped. The enemy floated the *Raleigh* again and took her into their navy.

The Continental Navy frigate *Confederacy* taking on stores

The connotation of the names *Alliance* and *Confederacy* being so similar would possibly indicate that the Marine Committee meant these ships to be the same—sister ships constructed from the same plan. The Congressional Resolution of November 20, 1776, authorized the construction of five 36-gun ships, but only these two were built. They were laid down at the same time, but the *Alliance* was ready for sea first. William Vernon wrote to John Adams on December 17, 1778: "The ship building at Norwich and called the *Confederacy,* near ready to sail; she is a fine Frigate it is said exceeds the *Alliance* if possible."

She was in fact a finer ship than the *Alliance,* evidently on purpose. England, France, Holland, and Spain each had ships that might have been called showpieces—richly carved, painted, and gilded; handsomely finished and appointed, in the style of the last quarter of the eighteenth century. The new American nation needed to be on an equal footing with these nations, to have a warship of its own making that would vie with the best that the skill of Europe could produce and that would attract attention in every port of call.

To their graces of bravery and perseverance the Patriot founders of the United States added farsighted optimism, for they envisioned the representatives of their nation crossing the Atlantic in a state that would win the approbation of the great powers of the world. But the eye appeal of the *Confederacy* was to be backed by the power of her guns, and to assert herself as an ambassador, she had first to be a warship.

She was a bit larger than the *Alliance,* and about her there was the touch of grandeur of a magnificent seventeenth-century warship. It was in her lines; she was long and narrow with a pleasing stately shape. Also, she was about the last of the large ships to have ports for sweep oars between her gunports. Her spacious "Great Room" with more than eight feet of ceiling height, was reflected in her beautiful quarters and stern, both alive with carvings more in the style of Queen Anne than that of George III. Her headframes were extraordinarily graceful and sweeping. She was built as a 36-gun frigate, but she had the airs of a 74-gun two-decker, according to her record drawings. When she was captured by the H.B.M. ships *Orpheus* and *Roebuck,* she was taken to England and put in drydock at one of the Royal Navy's great shipworks, Deptford perhaps. There, everything about her from her keel to her top railings was measured, noted, and put down on paper as a working drawing—"taking off her lines," it was called—to be kept on file at the British Admiralty to this day.

Built by Jedidiah Willets at Norwich, Connecticut, the *Confederacy* was 186 feet long from tip to tip, and adding to this her bowsprit boom, made 241 feet of space that she would require at a dock. Her beam width was 37 feet; her draught of water was 16 feet.

She was built for 36 guns, but in the service of her own navy she had only 28 or 30. To get guns was a great problem for the Marine Committee. America had no foundries when the war started. The mother country did not look with favor on the colonies having the ability to cast guns. So, after 1776, plants that could smelt, refine, and cast a heavy twelve-pounder had to be built, methods devised, and workmen trained; 36 guns just could not be made to meet a sailing date deadline.

The frigate *Confederacy* passing Cape May

The Continental Navy frigate *Confederacy,* fine and handsome as she was, also was the navy's most ill-fated ship. She promised so much, but bad luck sailed with her. Because of the shortage of nearly all items not made of wood—cordage, sails, and guns—and a lack of money, a long time had been required to get her ready for sea duty. She first sailed on a short cruise, commanded by Captain Seth Harding, one of the navy's most reliable officers. He had been the master of the Connecticut State Navy brig *Defence* when she put up a gallant fight in capturing a British troop transport; later he commanded a successful letter of marque vessel until receiving this new naval commission.

Next, the *Confederacy* was ordered to take the Honorable John Jay, Minister Plenipotentiary to Spain, to his post. With him were his wife, his brother-in-law, Brockholst Livingston, as private secretary, and M. Gérard, minister from France, returning home. The ship departed from Chester, Pennsylvania, on October 26, 1779. She was to avoid all other ships to reduce the risk of combat while the important passengers were aboard, and she was routed to go to Spain or France by a southern course. The captain had been given a dozen things to do when he arrived in France.

But Captain Harding wrote in his report; "Nov. 7 at five o'clock in the morning, in latitude 41°-3′, longitude 50°-39′, the ship unfortunately lost her Bow Sprit, Foremast, Main Mast and Mizzen Mast" in a gale. Six hours were required to cut away the wreckage and get up jury masts and sail. "But the next day about 7 o'clock A.M. in addition to our misfortune we found the Rudder to be gone, at least the head of it Wrung in such a manner that rendered it entirely useless, in which situation we lay Tossing and Drifting with the Wind and Current, making use of every Opportunity to secure the Rudder and Refit the Ship in order to proceed on her intended Passage till the 23d November."

The *Confederacy* had drifted eastward and was now at longitude 48° 28′. "I with the advice of Mr. Jay and Mr. Gerard, Call'd a Council of my Officers Relative to the ship proceeding on her intended passage who unanimously agreed that it would be very imprudent to approach the Coast of Europe in the situation she was then in; that it would be impossible for the Rudder to survive a hard Gale of wind without increasing the Leake Very much, which was occasioned by the Rudder's striking the stern post. . . ."

The ship had been hit by a freak storm, a spawning hurricane. And one thing that shipwrights had to learn about large ships such as the *Confederacy* was that rigging that seemed taut in a dry northern climate slackened in the moist southern air.

It was a masterful job of seafaring to get the distressed ship into Saint-Pierre, Martinique, under jury sail. She landed on December 18. Her passengers went to France on a French frigate. The *Confederacy* took months to be refitted to be able to return to Philadelphia on May 1, 1780. After considerable repair work she cruised in the Delaware with the frigate *Boston.* This was the only untroubled naval service of the fine ship.

In the early spring of 1781, with the *Deane* and *Saratoga,* she went to the West Indies. She was returning home with these frigates and a large convoy of French and American merchantmen. All were heavily laden, none more than the *Confederacy,* when she fell in with H.B.M. ships *Roebuck,* 44 guns, and *Orpheus,* 32 guns. In face of such superior force the captain decided that resistance was useless and struck his flag, thus ending her service. In the Royal Navy she was renamed the *Confederate.*

The Continental Navy frigate *Providence*

The Continental Navy frigate *Providence*, 28 guns, was one of the original thirteen authorized by the Continental Congress and with the frigate *Warren* perhaps the first to be completed. They were built in Providence, Rhode Island. Difficulty in recruiting crews to man them and the occupation of Newport and the lower Narragansett Bay by the British kept them in port until late spring of 1778.

Early in March of 1778, the frigate *Warren* successfully ran the blockade of the British fleet in Narragansett Bay and got to sea. Next to attempt this perilous feat was the *Providence*. William Vernon wrote to John Adams: "The 30th of April we sent her down and she succeeded. Capt. Whipple, having on hand about 170 men, who was ordered to the first port in France he could make, to be under the direction of the Commissioners, where we hope she is safe arrived. No dispatches was sent by this ship, as she was to pass a dangerous passage; however, in a brisk Wind & dark Night she got out safe, receiving a heavy fire from the *Lark* which was the uppermost ship, who's Fires he returned with Spirit & good effect, Killed a Number & Wounded many men, much disabled the Ship: the lower most ship by this alarm was prepared to receive the *Providence* who was obliged to pass her very near, gave her their Fire, that was returned with good success."

Having reached the open sea, the *Providence* did not stop until she was in French waters.

With the *Boston* and the *Ranger* the two ships sailed back to America, arriving at Portsmouth on October 15 with four prizes.

The *Queen of France, Ranger,* and *Providence* went on a cruise in June, 1779. Captain Whipple was the senior officer. A midshipman on the *Queen* made an account of this unique voyage in which the Americans fell in with a Jamaica fleet of 150 sails near the Banks of Newfoundland. Nothing could be seen, but the sound of guns and ships' bells told the presence of a fleet. When the fog lifted a bit before noon, the *Queen* found herself near a large merchantman from whom it was learned that the fleet was under convoy of a 74-gun vessel and five frigates, plus some sloops of war. Under the pretense of being a British frigate, the *Queen* sent one of her boats to the merchant ship and quietly took possession of her. She then took another the same way. Captain Whipple first feared that his ships would be detected and captured, but since no alarm was given joined in the game. At the end of the day the Americans had taken eleven fat prizes from the fleet and returned to port with nine of them.

The *Providence* went on two patrol cruises, and with the *Queen of France* and the *Ranger* sailed from Nantasket Roads, south of Boston, on November 23, 1779, under secret orders. They cruised eastward to Bermuda, where they were hit by a thirty-hour gale of such force as to spring the mizzen masts of the *Providence* and *Ranger.* Their goal was the defense of Charleston, where all three were captured, taken into the Royal Navy, and sent to Halifax, Nova Scotia. The *Providence* was sold out at the end of the war. We have no further record of her.

The frigate *Saratoga* capturing the *Charming Molly*

The last important naval measure by the Congress for the year 1776 was the Act of November 20, resolving to build three 74-gun ships, five 36-gun frigates, an 18-gun brig, and a packet boat. This list was so modified by the work actually done that the stipulations of the act were only partially fulfilled. One of the frigates built and got to sea was the Continental Navy sloop of war *Saratoga,* 18 guns. Captain John Young, her only commander, had been the master of the sloop *Independence,* 10 guns. This vessel had been steady in duty, making a voyage to France for supplies. She was captured in the spring of 1777, but her captain was freed on a prisoner of war exchange.

The dimensions of the *Saratoga* are not known, except that she was about the same size as the *Ranger,* though a better-looking and a better ship. Built at Philadelphia by the famous Wharton and Humphreys shipyard in 1777, she got away before the city fell to the British forces, and was taken to a New England port to be fitted out.

Not much was heard of her until June, 1780, when she made up part of a force to cruise by order of the Admiralty Board—the new Anglicized and fashionable name for the old Marine Committee. On this cruise the *Saratoga* captured four valuable prizes. In mid-October she was prowling the Atlantic shipping lanes when she fell in with three enemy sails—a ship and two brigs. The ship was the *Charming Molly,* a heavily armed merchantman, bound for New York from Bristol; she had almost twice the size and arms of the American ship.

The brigs scattered to stand off when the *Saratoga* ranged up to the enemy ship, and on hailing, she showed the Continental flag. The enemy started firing and the American answered with what guns could be brought to bear, as she was to the windward and a bit astern. She kept moving up on the Englishman.

Captain Young now held his fire until he had run alongside, his hull giving the merchant ship a sound bump. At the same time he opened up with his forward guns in a sheet of fire pointblank, followed immediately by a boarding party of fifty men. Led by the fearless young Joshua Barney, they jumped fighting to the English deck. A boat from the American ship had also been got out, and her men were soon climbing onto the English deck through a war-damaged gunport.

One of the enemy brigs now came up and got into the fight by firing a few shots, but lost heart when she received a few from the *Saratoga* in turn. She sheered off and vanished.

The Americans on board the *Charming Molly* overpowered the crew, hauled down her flags, and took her as a prize. Captain Young put her under command of Lieutenant Barney to send her to Boston. That night the *Charming Molly* was retaken by H.M.S. *Iris,* and Lieutenant Barney and his men were sent to Plymouth, England, to the infamous Mill Prison. This was the third time this young man had been a British prisoner. He had been exchanged once, escaped once, and now, despite close detention and confinement, he escaped again. He made his way by packet boat to the coast of France where he was discovered and returned to the same confinement. He, with five other Americans, escaped again, made their way across England, to Holland, to France, and home, where he was to be one of the heroes of the navy.

The sloop of war *Saratoga* was never reported again. She was presumed lost at sea.

The *General Pickering* in battle with the *Achilles*

The American privateer *General Pickering,* with 16 six-pounder guns, was from the port of Salem, Massachusetts. In 1780 she sailed under Captain Jonathan Haraden of Salem with a crew of fifty-two on a voyage to Spain. On May 29 she fell in with a Royal Navy 16-gun cutter and beat her off after a two-hour action. Three days later in the Bay of Biscay she captured an enemy schooner, the *Golden Eagle,* 14 guns, with a crew of fifty-seven. The prize was sent to Bilbao where the *General Pickering* herself was headed. On going into the harbor she could not avoid the *Achilles,* an armed merchantman out of London, nearly three times the size of the American ship. The English ship carried 22 nine-pounders and 18 other guns. Her crew was 130 men.

This large ship showed a disposition to fight despite the fact that she was in Spanish waters. Captain Haraden, renowned for his exploits in taking prizes as commander of the privateer *Tyrannicide,* quickly sized up the enemy. From his lifetime as a mariner he knew that his ship's qualities were such that he could sail rings around the dull Londoner, and that was precisely what he did. He put his helm down and came up under the enemy's stern, firing each gun in turn as he passed her; then he circled her wide and came up to her bow to do the same. Next he came about and repeated the maneuver in reverse, and the third time he fired all his guns into both the *Achilles'* sides. The *Achilles* dropped her main courses, sheered off, and sailed away.

This had happened on a cloudless, beautiful summer day with a fair wind quartering onshore. The firing had attracted the citizens of Bilbao, and thousands lined the coast to watch. A number wanting to get a better look came out in boats and all but got into the fight themselves.

When the *General Pickering* got into port at Bilbao, she was greeted like a hero toreador. The people would have it no other way but that Captain Haraden had put on a fight just for them. The *General Pickering* was pretty badly cut up and several times hulled. She was repaired, refitted, and on August 1 set out for home. These are the entries from the ship's log by the captain on the return voyage:

"August 5th All Light sails out. At 3 P.M. took in St. g sails. The Dutchmen in sight. Also discovered another sail to Windward. 4 P.M. She bore down upon us—got all ready for engaging—at 8 P.M. lost sight of her.

"August 6th Saw a brigg on our Lee Quarter; like wise a cutter in chase of us under our Lee Quarter. August 7th 8 A.M. Saw a Sail ahead which appears to be a large ship. 10 A.M. took in St. g sails and hauled our wind Merd., she backed and gave us chase.

"August 8th The ship in chace rather gains on us—All sail out which we can set upon a wind.

"At 5 A.M. saw the ship on our Lee quarter, haul'd to, to keep all sails drawing—she haul'd to after us 10 A.M. bore away before the wind. Light breezes. Got out our Oars and Row'g rather gain from her.

"August 9th The ship still in chace and we keep on Row'g 7 P.M. She haul'd to Southw'd—we left off Rowing."

The *General Pickering* arrived in Salem September 14. She brought two English brigs as prizes, one taken August 28, the other September 3.

The *Protector* in battle with the *Admiral Duff*

The hotbed of Loyalists who had made their home at the British-held Penobscot River were a troublesome lot to Massachusetts, and that state launched an expedition to capture the area. But it ended in total failure, with the terrible loss of three large Massachusetts State Navy vessels. It was fortunate that the 26-gun *Protector* being built and outfitted on the Merrimack River was not ready for sea. Had she been, she too would have gone on the expedition and perhaps would have been lost.

The *Protector* sailed with Captain Williams in command. One of his midshipmen was Edward Preble, afterward to be one of the very famous names of the United States Navy. On a cruise the *Protector* fought a hard battle off the Newfoundland banks with a British ship, the *Admiral Duff*, 32 guns, on June 9, 1780. When first sighted she was taken for a frigate, but this did not deter Captain Williams from ranging up to her. An account of this naval action by one of the crew is known as the "Narrative of Luther Little."

"When the fog lifted, saw large ship to windward under English colors, standing before the wind for us, we being to leeward. Looked as large as a 74. Concluded she was not a frigate. All hands piped to quarters. Hammocks brought and stuffed in the nettings, decks wet and sanded, etc. . . .

"We stood on under cruising sail. She tried to go ahead of us and then hove to under fighting sail. We showed English flag. She was preparing for action. We steered down across her stern and hauled up under her lee quarter, breeching our guns aft to bring them to bear. Our first lieutenant hailed from the gangboard. . . .

"Our captain ordered broadside and colors changed. She replied with three cheers and a broadside. Being higher, they overshot us, cutting our rigging. A regular fight within pistol range. In a half hour a cannon shot came through our side, killing Mr. Scollay, a midshipman who commanded the fourth 14-pounder from the stern. His brains flew over my face and my gun, which was the third from the stern.

"In an hour all their topmen were killed by our marines, sixty in number and all Americans. Our marines killed the man at their wheel, and the ship came down on us, her cat-head staving in our quarter galley. We lashed their jibboom to our main shrouds. Our marines firing into the port holes kept them from charging. We were ordered to board, but the lashing broke and we were ordered back. Their ship shooting alongside narly locked our guns and we gave a broadside, which cut away her mizenmast and made great havoc. Saw her sinking and her main topgallant sail on fire, which run down her rigging and caught a hogshead of cartridges under her quarter deck and blew it off.

"A charge of grape entered my port hole. One passed between my backbone and windpipe and one through my jaw, lodging in the roof of my mouth and taking off a piece of my tongue, the other through my upper lip, taking away part and all my upper teeth. Was carried to cockpit; my gun was fired only once after. I had fired it nineteen times. Thinking I was mortally wounded, they dressed first those likelier to live. Heard the surgeon say, 'He will die.'

"The *Duff* sunk, on fire, colors flying. Our boats had been injured, but were repaired as well as possible and sent to pick up the swimmers; saved fifty-five, one half wounded. Their first lieutenant confided to me that many were drowned rather than be made captives. Some tried to jump from the boats. Our surgeons amputated limbs of five of them. One was sick with West India fever and had floated out of his hammock between decks. The weather was warm and in less than ten days sixty of our men had it. Among those saved were two American captains and their crews, prisoners on board the *Duff*. One of the American captains told us that Captain [Richard] Stranger [commander of the *Admiral Duff*] had hoped we were a Continental frigate when he first saw us."

A fight to a draw, the *Trumbull* and the *Watt*

Each of the frigates built or started for the Continental Navy presented its own problem, but that of the *Trumbull*, 28 guns, was unique. She was one of the original thirteen, constructed according to the Act of Congress on December 13, 1775. Built on the Connecticut River at Chatham, this frigate was launched in the summer of 1776. But that is as far as she got for two years, because a bar had formed at the mouth of the river and she could not get over it.

There was constant fear that the British would make a raid to burn this vessel, and for the two years that she was captive in the river, an armed guard of some force was maintained.

Many schemes were proposed to get over the bar; the one employed was put forth by Captain Hinman. Two hundred barrels were filled with water. They were tied in twos on the ends of ropes which were tightly passed under the ship's keel. Then the water was pumped from the barrels, buoying up the hull, and the ships floated over the bar, out to sea, down to New London to be fitted out.

It was not until April, 1780, that she was ready to go to sea. Captain James Nicholson was given her command. He had been the captain of the *Virginia* when she was lost aground. Late in May the *Trumbull* sailed and had been at sea only a few days when she fell in with the British letter of marque, the ship *Watt*, 26 guns. Apart from the battle between the *Bon Homme Richard* and H.B.M. *Serapis*, this was the fiercest naval fight of the war. It came to a draw. The captains of both vessels gave detailed reports of the action; though the men were unknown to each other, their accounts are much the same. The letter of Gilbert Saltonstall, captain of the Marines on board the *Trumbull*, reads:

"As soon as she discovered us she bore down for us. We got ready for action, at one o'clock began to engage, and continued without the least intermission for five glasses, within pistol shot. It is beyond my power to give an adequate idea of the carnage, slaughter, havoc and destruction that ensued. We were literally cut all to pieces; not a shroud, stay, brace bowline or any other of our rigging standing. Our main top mast shot away, our fore, main and mizzen masts gone by the board, two of our quarter-deck guns disabled, thro' our ensign 62 shot, our mizzen 157, main sail 560, foresail 180, our other sails in proportion. Not a yard in the ship but received one or more shot, six shot through her quarter above the quarter deck, four in the waste, our quarter, stern and nettings full of langrage, grape and musket ball. We suffered more than we otherwise should on account of the ship that engaged us being a very dull sailer. Our ship being out of command, she kept on our starboard quarter the latter part of the engagement. After two and a half hours action she hauld her wind, her pumps going; we edged away so that it may fairly be called a drawn battle."

The *Watt* was not out of sight of the *Trumbull* when her shattered mainmast went by the board.

The troubles aboard the *Trumbull* did not cease with the engagement. The decks were cleared of wreckage, and jury sail was got up, but a blinding gale of wind and rain hit her and took all away again, then another the next day and the next. She limped back to port.

She was repaired and went to sea twice more on useful cruises. On the third cruise she fought a 24-gun privateer and was about to take her when her mainmast fell and she was disabled. The enemy escaped. She herself was captured that same night by H.M.S. *Iris*, the former *Hancock*.

Continental Navy frigates overtaking an enemy fleet

On March 13, 1779, the Continental Navy frigates *Warren*, under Captain Hopkins, *Queen of France*, under Captain Olney, and *Ranger*, under Captain Simpsen, sailed in company from Boston. Captain Hopkins was the senior officer. The journal of the *Ranger* has an entry of interest for April 6: "At 6 A.M., saw 2 sails, gave Chase to one of them; at ½ past 6 the *Warren* and *Queen* hois'd English Colors and fired a gun Leeward, as did we, which she answered and bro't too at 7. We brought too, found her to be the *Hibernia*, a Schooner of 10 guns, a British Privateer; sent 2 of Our People on Board to help man her."

From seamen captured on this vessel it was found out that a fleet of armed transports and storeships had sailed from New York, bound for Georgia with supplies for the enemy's forces. The *Hibernia* and the other sail, both part of the fleet, had fallen behind.

The American crowded sail in chase. Resuming the *Ranger*'s journal: "The next morning at ½ past 5 saw a fleet of 9 sails to the N.E. at 6 made sail and gave chase, at 8 tacked Ship by Signal and made all Sail we could, alow and aloft; found we gained on the Fleet, our Consort the *Warren* out-sailing us all. . . . In the afternoon —pleasant gales and fair weather. The *Warren*, *Queen* and Ourselves in Chase of the Fleet; at 4 P.M. came up with them."

After a feeble resistance from the armed vessels, the fleet surrendered except two. Favored by the oncoming darkness, they escaped. Those captured were the ship *Jason*, 20 guns, under Captain Porterfield, with 150 men, the convoy to the fleet; the ship *Maria*, a letter of marque, 16 guns, eighty-four men, very richly laden with provisions, dry goods, and harness for a regiment of horse and arms; the brigs *Patriot*, *Prince Ferdinand*, *John*, and *Batchelor;* and the schooner *Chance* with a sizable cargo of army goods.

Among the passengers on board the *Jason* were a colonel, a lieutenant colonel, two captains, and two lieutenants, and a bandmaster. Aboard the brigs were mostly troop replacements.

The *Ranger*'s journal for April says: "Jogging along under easy sail, to keep our little fleet together, the *Patriot* being a slow heavy sailer, the *Warren* at 7 took her in tow."

Captain Hopkins gave his report of the cruise, much the same as the journal of the *Ranger*, concluding with: "On the 16th instant I arrived in this port [Boston] having parted with the fleet in thick fog. The next day the *Jason* arrived, which is a very fine ship; also the schooner at Portsmouth which is a very valuable vessel. Several Vessels are now in sight which I hope is some of the fleet. By the activity of Captains Olney and Simpsen we manned the fleet in five hours."

The *Queen of France* made port in Boston several days after the *Warren* and the *Jason*, bringing with her the *Maria*. The two other prizes were taken to Portsmouth by the *Ranger* on April 21.

The *Jason* and *Hibernia* were fitted out as American privateers. The former had an astounding career.

The Marine Committee was greatly pleased with the results of the cruise and sent congratulations to Captain Hopkins.

The *Congress* in engagement with the H.M.S. *Savage*

Captain Stirling of the Royal Navy reported the capture of his ship in a letter dated September 23, 1781:

"It is with the most poignant grief I acquaint your Excellency of the capture of his Majesty's sloop *Savage* late under my command. . . . Early in the morning, 10 leagues East of Charlestown, we espied a ship bearing down on us, who when about four miles distant, hauled her wind to the Eastward, showing by her appearance she was an American cruizer; her force could not be so easily distinguished. I gave way to the pleasing idea that she was a privateer carrying 20 nine pounders, and instantly resolved either to bring her to action or oblige her to quit the coast, for which purpose we gave chase, but were prevented continuing it long by her edging down, seemingly determined to engage us. Conscious of our superiority in sailing and force, this maneuver coincided with my wishes. I caused the *Savage* to lay by till we perceived on her nearer approach she was far superior to what we imagined and that it was necessary to attempt making our escape.

"At half past ten she began firing bow chasers and at eleven, being close on our quarter, the action commenced with musquetry, which after a good deal of execution was followed by a heavy cannonade on both sides. In an hour's time I had the mortification to see our braces and bowlines shot away and not a rope left to trim the sail with, notwithstanding every precaution had been taken; however, our fire was so constant and well directed that the enemy did not see our situation, but kept alongside of us till accident obliged him to drop astern.

"The *Savage* was now almost a wreck, her sails, rigging and yards so much cut that it was with utmost difficulty we could alter our position time enough to avoid being raked, the enemy lying directly athwart our stern for some minutes. This was the only intermission of the great guns, but musquetry and pistols still did execution and continued till they opened again which was not till both ships were almost on board each other, when the battle became more furious than before. Our quarter deck and forecastle were soon now nearly cleared, scarce a man belonging to either not killed or wounded, with three guns on our main deck rendered useless. In this situation we fought near an hour with only five six-pounders, the fire from each ship's guns scorching the men who opposed them, shot and other implements of war thrown by hand. Our mizzen mast being shot away by the board, our main mast tottering with only three shrouds standing, the ship on fire dangerously, only 40 men on duty to oppose the foe who was attempting to board us in three places, no succor in sight or possibility of making further resistance, I was necessitated at a quarter before three P.M. to surrender."

The American was the *Congress*, a private ship of war belonging to merchants of Philadelphia, under the command of Captain Geddes.

Of her crew of 215 men, 8 were killed, 30 wounded. The ship was so damaged that she had to return to Charleston for repairs. During the battle the ships were never more than ninety feet apart, on a smooth sea in fair weather.

The losses on the *Savage* were thought to be much greater than on the *Congress*, and far more than were reported by Captain Stirling.

The frigate *South Carolina* in the Delaware River

The Continental Congress instructed the American commissioners in Paris to "build, buy or hire ships of the line, frigates and other war vessels." But they found that to buy or hire ships was not possible. The French minister, after hearing and considering the Americans' request, refused, explaining that her fleets could not be reduced at a time when war with England threatened. An appeal to Sweden was rejected, on the basis of doubtful credit. But in Holland the agents met with success. The proposal for that country to construct a ship for the Americans was agreed upon. A fine, 40-gun frigate was built at Amsterdam.

But when the ship was nearing completion, the government of Holland sold her to the King of France, giving as the reason some complex international involvement. At the bottom of all this was the real reason—an uncertainty that America could pay for the vessel. Somehow during the construction this ship had taken on a decidedly "French" look, and at completion was every inch a French ship, including her name—*Indien.*

For the Continental Navy not to have this fine new ship was a real loss, and Dr. Benjamin Franklin worked assiduously at trying to persuade the French to give her to his country. Captain John Paul Jones had set his heart on commanding this ship for the American cause. When he returned to France fresh from his victory of the *Ranger* against the *Drake,* he and Dr. Franklin made a concerted campaign to get the *Indien.* But their efforts failed, and they got instead the creaking old *Duc de Duras,* which was to become the *Bon Homme Richard.*

Commodore Alexander Gillow of South Carolina, in France in the interests of his state, by some arrangement never made clear, was able to lease the *Indien* for his state's navy, and for this service she was named the *South Carolina.* She was the largest frigate to fly the American flag. It was not an easy matter to get her from berth at Amsterdam, fitted out, and ready for sea, especially with the British watching each move and waiting for her. By some ruse Commodore Gillow got the Royal Navy to look the other way, and his ship went to sea in August, 1781. Within five days she had taken five prizes in the North Sea; from there went to the West Indies by way of Spain, and on December 31 was off Charleston, South Carolina. Finding the city in British hands, she returned at once to Havana.

With the Spanish governor, Commodore Gillow planned and carried out a raid on New Providence Island, in which he commanded the naval part of the expedition, with his frigate the flagship of a fleet of fifty-nine American and Spanish privateers. On May 5, 1782, they lay before the island, the flagship in gun range of Fort Nassau. Surrender demands were sent to the governor, and at length he capitulated. The success of the raid was credited to the Americans, who maneuvered their vessels through difficult passages to surprise the British.

The painting shows the *South Carolina* in the Delaware River on the way to Philadelphia, where she went, arriving on May 28, to remain six months. Command of this ship was given to Captain Joyner of the South Carolina Navy. She left Philadelphia with three ships on convoy bound for France. On entering the Atlantic from the Delaware Capes, they encountered three British Navy ships, the *Diomede,* 44 guns; the *Quebec,* 32 guns; and *Astrea,* 32 guns, which had been alerted from a spy report and were waiting. They attacked the *South Carolina* and after an hour-long fierce fight captured her. No account of the Continental Navy or the young American nation at sea warfare could overlook this interesting ship that could have done so much for the American cause in the Revolution and ended by doing so little.

The frigate *Deane* in a "cutting out" action

Perhaps it was because Silas Deane, the American confidential agent in France, was successful in purchasing for his country shiploads of supplies without the use of money that was also requested to purchase warships for the Continental Navy. He procured two, the frigates *Queen of France* and the *Deane,* so named because he was proud of the honor or because no one else would allow such a peculiar warship to bear his name.

The *Deane* had two decks, with 16 guns on each. She was not much more than 100 feet in length, and had a 32-foot beam. She carried 24 twelve-pounders, 6 four-pounders, 2 six-pounders, and plenty of cohorns and swivel guns.

In the late eighteenth century, supplying warships to the French government was partly a "speculative builder's" business. A contractor might put together a warship with innovations and improvements to appeal to the navy brass and sell his work to the nation. Or it might not sell. The *Deane* may have been a ship the French Navy did not want. It is said that a plan for her was submitted to the Congress, but no plan has ever been found in America or France. There is not a record that a ship of this type was ever contracted for or built by the navy of France.

But in the decade of the American Revolution, the British Navy experimented with 32-gun frigates about the same size as the *Deane*. Those built must not have proven to be worthwhile, for they were remodeled from two decks of 16 guns each to one deck of 14 guns. From the record plans in the British Admiralty an idea can be gained as to how the frigate *Deane* may have looked in her day.

Silas Deane could have seen in this ship just what his country needed—a power package at a cut-rate price; firepower to equal a frigate twice the size. Also, she sailed with a much smaller crew than a larger ship, and manpower was a real problem in America. Captain Samuel Nicholson was her very successful commander for most of her service, which started from Nantes where she was built. Her crew of seventy was hidden to prevent the British ambassador from knowing that she was ready to go to sea. She arrived in Boston May, 1778. Until the following winter that harbor was blockaded and she did not get out until January 14. On her second day she fought and captured and sent back to Boston a valuable prize, the *Viper,* 16 guns, seventy-five men. She also burned a London ship. She took six prizes in the West Indies before returning to Philadelphia on April 17, 1779. After leaving on July 1, she captured eight vessels. Sailing from the Chesapeake on July 27, she took eight more. With the frigate *Boston* she captured the enemy ships *Sandwich* and *Thorn.*

It was always the same: the *Deane* was ready to follow orders, cruise wherever directed, was seldom hurt or wounded, gave only the enemy trouble, and paid for herself several times over with enemy prizes captured. Then Silas Deane fell from glory and the Congress changed the name of the vessel to the *Hague.* Also, for reasons never made clear, the command of the frigate was placed in other hands. The *Hague* was never the same warship as the *Deane,* and she was sold out of the service before the war ended.

The frigate *Alliance,* favorite of the Continental Navy

The surrender of General Cornwallis at Yorktown almost closed the military operations on land of the American Revolutionary War, but hostilities at sea continued. Although the Continental Navy was about exhausted, the privateers and state navies carried on their activity with telling vigor.

General Washington and the Congress agreed that Lafayette must again present the plight of the United States to the French court, and Captain Barry was ordered to take him to France on the frigate *Alliance.* Barry and Lafayette landed there on January 18, 1782. Captain Barry had avoided all enemy vessels on this crossing, his third. The *Alliance* was back at New London, Connecticut, on May 18, and after a stay at port, she sailed on a cruise on August 4. She captured a brig, a schooner, a sloop, a whaler brig, a Jamaica brig loaded with rum and sugar, and two ships. She landed again in France at L'Orient. For the fourth time she left France for home by way of Martinique, There the captain found orders to proceed to Havana to bring to the United States a large amount of specie and to sail in company with a ship that had been purchased for the Continental Navy, the *Duc de Lauzon.*

The ships departed Havana on March 6, 1783, and four days out they fell in with three sails showing the enemy flag—the frigates H.M.S. *Alarm* and H.M.S. *Sybil,* and the sloop H.M.S. *Tobago.* It was a dark day, the *Duc de Lauzon* was a dull sailer, and to keep near her the *Alliance* was under reefed sail. The *Alarm* was in the van. She ranged up to the *Alliance* to hail. The American answered with her flag, and the firing started from each ship, fast and hot. The other two enemy vessels were directing their course toward the *Lauzon,*

and Captain Barry, having in mind how slow she was, signaled her to heave her guns, boats, and all else overboard and run.

The *Alarm,* evidently hurt by the *Alliance's* fire, sheered off and shortened sail as if to withdraw from the action. At this, Captain Barry had his ship drop astern of the *Lauzon* so that he would be between her and the *Sybil,* now coming up fast and near. This movement placed the *Alliance* at about pistol range from the enemy. The darkness and rough sea would make gun aim hit or miss, and Captain Barry went from gun to gun instructing the crews how and when to fire. "Not too much haste," he admonished.

The firing started, broadsides from the *Sybil,* broadsides from the *Alliance* as they ran along almost side by side. Aim was difficult, rapid fire was not in order. Fire from the *Alliance* was more effective than that directed at her, but all was with rage and fury from the decks and the swivels and muskets from the tops. This running battle continued for over a glass, then only musket fire was coming from the enemy. The *Sybil* hoisted Call for Assistance flags but her companions were a good way behind. The enemy seemed inclined to sheer off; Captain Barry could not afford to get too far from the *Lauzon.*

This is considered the last engagement of the Continental Navy. The two Americans were separated in a storm off Cape Hatteras; the *Alliance* was chased by two enemy 74-gun ships off the Delaware capes.

The *Duc de Lauzon* arrived in Philadelphia on March 21; the *Alliance* had come in the day before. She went up to Providence; her crew was paid off. This was the end of the first navy.

The *Alliance* in the last naval action of the American Revolution

The Continental Navy frigate *Alliance*, 36 guns, was such a favorite that for many years there was a song about her that the people back in the mountains sang. The words became twisted and meaningless until only an expert in country folk music could determine what it was about.

The first part of this ship's life was not useful to the American cause of liberty and freedom. This was when she was under the command of Captain Pierre Landais, an experienced, former French naval officer who had served under the famous Admiral Bougainville. He had been recommended to Silas Deane, who in turn presented him to the Continental Congress for appointment as a captain. His first orders as captain of this ship were to take General Lafayette to France. Then his ship was added to the squadron commanded by Captain John Paul Jones for a cruise around the British Isles with the *Bon Homme Richard*. When the *Richard* and the *Serapis* were engaged in combat, Captain Landais on the *Alliance* fired many rounds into his American consort, for which action he would give no explanation. He was summarily dismissed from the service, but was reinstated with the aid of Arthur Lee and John Adams, and command of the *Alliance* was returned to him for a homeward voyage to America. On this crossing his conduct became so erratic as to endanger ship and crew, and he was forcibly relieved of command.

Captain John Barry was assigned command of the *Alliance* on September 5, 1780, and until the war's ending the ship was in constant and successful employment. The first orders for her new captain were to make another trip to France at General Washington's urgent request, to raise money for his army and enlist the aid of the French Navy. She left L'Orient for the return home March 29, 1781.

The next day a plot by Englishmen in the crew to capture the ship and take her to England was discovered and put down with strong measures. Two days later the British brigs H.M.S. *Mars*, 22 guns, 112 men; and H.M.S. *Minerva*, 10 guns, attacked the *Alliance*. Both vessels were captured. Then, two merchant brigs were captured. Next, lightning struck her mainmast, splitting the topmast.

On May 28, she sighted two sails standing directly for her. This was late in the day; they followed through the night and were seen astern the next morning. It was a cloudless, almost windless day with only enough air astir to move these light vessels, while the *Alliance* lay like a log in the water. Owing to the lack of wind, it was almost noon before the ships ranged up, showing British colors. They opened fire. The American fired in return, but, motionless, she was a perfect target for the two lighter enemy vessels. Captain Barry was struck in the shoulder by grapeshot and had to be carried below. With his wounds bound, he attempted to direct the order of the ship from his bed. The *Alliance* was being hurt by the two British war vessels, and when her flagpole was struck and the American colors fell into the sea, the customary cheer of victory went up from the British.

But the *Alliance* was a happy and lucky ship. A squall line of wind and rain which had been seen scooting across the calm sea at that moment reached the *Alliance*, filled her sails, and gave her life. Now she could deal with the enemy, and her fire stung like a hornet. It was not too long before she had captured H.M.S. *Trepasy*, 14 guns, and H.M.S. *Atalanta*, 16 guns.

Sources

ALLEN, GARDNER W., *A Naval History of the American Revolution.* Boston, Houghton Mifflin, 1913.

BARNES, JOHN S., *The Logs of the Serapis—Alliance—Ariel Under the Command of John Paul Jones, 1779–80.* New York, printed for the Naval History Society by the DeVinne Press, 1911.

CHAPELLE, HOWARD I., *The History of the American Sailing Navy.* New York, Norton, 1949.

————, *The Search for Speed Under Sail.* New York, Norton, 1967.

COOPER, JAMES FENIMORE, *History of the Navy of the United States of America.* Philadelphia, Lea & Blanchard, 1839.

CUTLER, CARL C., *Greyhounds of the Sea.* Annapolis, U.S. Naval Institute, 1930.

MACKENZIE, ALEXANDER S., *The Life of John Paul Jones.* Boston, Hilliard, Gray & Co., 1841.

MORISON, SAMUEL ELIOT, *John Paul Jones: A Sailor's Biography.* Boston, Little, Brown, 1959.

Naval Documents of the American Revolution, Vols. I–IV. Washington, U.S. Government Printing Office.

SHERBURNE, JOHN HENRY, *The Life and Character of John Paul Jones.* New York, Adriance, Sherman & Co., 1851.